Lotus® 1-2-3® Release 2.2

QUICK REFERENCE HANDBOOK
SECOND EDITION

Lotus® 1-2-3® Release 2.2

QUICK REFERENCE HANDBOOK
SECOND EDITION

Karen Cuneo
Gary Bond

C P C E
Center for Professional Computer Education

John Wiley & Sons, Inc.
New York • Chichester • Brisbane • Toronto • Singapore

Recognizing the importance of preserving what has been written, it is a policy of John Wiley & Sons, Inc. to have books of enduring value published in the United States printed on acid-free paper, and we exert our best efforts to that end.

Lotus and 1-2-3 are registered trademarks of Lotus Development Corporation.

This publication is designed to provide accurate and authoritative information in regard to the subject matter covered. It is sold with the understanding that the publisher is not engaged in rendering legal, accounting, or other professional service. If legal advice or other expert assistance is required, the services of a competent professional person should be sought. FROM A DECLARATION OF PRINCIPLES JOINTLY ADOPTED BY A VOMMITTEE OF THE AMERICAN BAR ASSOCIATION AND A COMMITTEE OF PUBLISHERS.

Copyright © 1986, 1990 by John Wiley & Sons, Inc.

All rights reserved. Published simultaneously in Canada.

Reproduction or translation of any part of this work beyond that permitted by section 107 or 108 of the 1976 United States Copyright Act without the permission of the copyright owner is unlawful. Requests for permission Department, John Wiley & Sons, Inc.

Library of Congress Cataloging-in-Publication Data

Cuneo, Karen.
   Lotus 1-2-3 release 2.2 : quick reference handbook / Karen Cuneo. Gary Bond. — 2nd ed.
     p. cm.
   "CPCE, Center for Professional Computer Education."
   Rev. ed. of: Lotus 1-2-3 quick reference handbook / Gary C. Bond. Karen Cuneo. c1986.
   Includes bibliographical references and index.
   ISBN 0-471-51679-1
   1. Lotus 1-2-3 (Computer program) 2. Business—Data processing.
I. Bond, Gary C. II. Bond, Gary C. Lotus 1-2-3 quick reference handbook. III. CPCE (Organization) IV. Title. V. Title: Lotus one -two-three release 2.2
HF5548.4.L67B66 1990
650'.0285'5369—dc20   90-12591
                                                                                 CIP

Printed in the United States of America
90 91 10 9 8 7 6 5 4 3 2 1

INTRODUCTION

The Lotus 1-2-3 software package is a very powerful tool that runs on many different computer systems. Although Lotus 1-2-3 is basically the same no matter what system it runs on, there may be some minor differences from one system to another. This was taken into consideration when this handbook was written. However, if you have difficulty with any of the information contained within this handbook, refer to your system's Lotus 1-2-3 or DOS manual.

Although this handbook contains quite a bit of explanatory information about the Lotus 1-2-3 program, it is NOT a training program. It is a reference guide for those people who have already received some training on Lotus 1-2-3.

This Quick Reference Handbook is arranged so that you can easily access exactly the information you are looking for. It is set up in four primary sections:

I. MENUS/SCREENS—This section contains a diagram of Access System Menu and the primary Screens that appear when Lotus is used. Part I begins on page M-1.

II. COMMAND LISTINGS—This section contains an alphabetical listing of all Lotus commands. It also contains a page number on which further information about the command can be found. Part II begins on page C-1.

III. REFERENCE GUIDE—This is the main body of the book. Here you will find detailed instructions on the operation of each aspect of Lotus 1-2-3.

IV. INDEX—This is a fully cross-referenced alphabetical index of Lotus 1-2-3 commands, features and functions. The index begins on page I-1.

CONTENTS

Part I Menus/Screens
ACCESS SYSTEM MENU	M–3
WORKSHEET GRID	M–4
/WORKSHEET STATUS SCREEN	M–5
/WORKSHEET GLOBAL SCREEN	M–6
/WORKSHEET GLOBAL DEFAULTS SCREEN ..	M–7
/PRINT (Printer or File) SCREEN	M–8
/GRAPH SCREEN	M–9
PRINTGRAPH MENU	M–10

Part II Commands
ACCESS SYSTEM MENU COMMANDS	C–3
1-2-3 WORKSHEET COMMANDS	C–5
1-2-3 RANGE COMMANDS	C–10
1-2-3 FILE COMMANDS	C–12
1-2-3 PRINT COMMANDS	C–14
1-2-3 GRAPH COMMANDS	C–16
1-2-3 DATA COMMANDS	C–18
1-2-3 ADD-IN COMMANDS	C–20
1-2-3 MISCELLANEOUS COMMANDS	C–20

Part III Reference Guide
GENERAL INFORMATION	3
Menus	3
Command Structure	3
Specifying a Range	4
Name—F3	5
ESC Key	6

Help — F1	6
Disk Handling	7
Write-Protect	8
SYSTEM STARTUP	9
Installation	9
System Startup	9
Lotus Access System Menu	10
Quit 1-2-3 — /Q	11
Temporarily Exit to Operating System — /S	11
Exit System — E	12
SCREEN ORIENTATION	13
Control Panel	13
Worksheet Grid	15
Scrolling	16
Cell Pointer Movement	16
Function Keys	17
GoTo — F5	18
Range Search — /RS	18
INPUT	19
Typing Information on the Worksheet	19
Error Correction	19
Typing Labels	20
Label Prefixes	21
Repeating Label	22
Compose — ALT+F1	23
Typing Values	24
Typing Formulas	24
Absolute Values	26
SUM Formula Construction	27
BUILT-IN FUNCTIONS	28
Date and Time Functions	28
Financial Functions	30
Mathematical Functions	32
Statistical Functions	34
String Functions	35
Logical Functions	39
Special Functions	40

CONTENTS

FORMATTING 45
   Format Commands 45
   Global Format — /WGF 45
   Range Format — /RF 46
   Format Menu Selections 47
   Fixed Format 48
   Scientific Format 48
   Currency Format 49
   Comma (,) Format 49
   General Format 50
   Horizontal Bar Graph (+/-) Format 50
   Percent Format 50
   Date Format 51
   Text Format 52
   Hidden Format 52
   Reset Format 52
   Range Label-Prefix — /RL 52
   Global Label-Prefix — /WGL 53
   Zero Suppression — /WGZ 54
   Range Justify — /RJ 55
   Column Width (Individual Columns) — /WC . 56
   Column Width (Range of Columns) — /WCC . 57
   Global Column Width — /WGC 58
   Hide/Display Columns — /WCH, /WCD 59
   Titles Command — /WT 60
   Window Command — /WW 61
   Global Worksheet Protection — /WGP 62
   Range Unprotect/Protect — /RU, /RP 63
EDITING 64
   General Information 64
   Erase Worksheet — /WE 64
   Delete Column/Row — /WD 65
   Range Erase — /RE 66
   Insert Column/Row — /WI 67
   Copy — /C 68
   Range Value — /RV 68
   Range Transpose — /RT 69

Move — /M	70
Specifying "Copy To" and "Move To" Range	71
Undo — ALT+F4	72
Disable/Enable Undo — /WGDOU	72
Range Search — /RS(F,L,B)F	73
Range Search and Replace — /RS(F,L,B)R	74
STORAGE	76
Save File — /FS	76
Retrieve File — /FR	78
Combine Files — /FC	79
File Xtract — /FX	81
List Files — /FL	83
File Directory — /FD	83
File Erase — /FE	84
File Import — /FI	86
File Tables — /FAT	87
Linking Files	88
Refresh Link — /FAL	89
Set File Reservation — /FAR	89
TRANSLATE FILES	91
PRINTING	94
The Print Command — /P	94
Print Menu Selections	95
Print Options Menu Selections	95
Print Default Settings	97
Calculating Left and Right Margins	97
Setting Left and Right Margins — /P(P,F)OM(L,R)	97
Calculating Top and Bottom Margins	98
Setting Top and Bottom Margins — /P(P,F)OM(T,B-)	99
Page Length — /P(P,F)OP	100
Page Break — /WP	101
Header/Footer — /P(P,F)O(H,F)	101
Printer Setup Strings — /P(P,F)OS	103
Clear Print Options — /P(P,F)C	104
Clear Margins — /P(P,F)OMN	105

CONTENTS

- Cancel Printing — CTRL+BREAK 106
- Allways Add-In 106
- MISCELLANEOUS 108
  - Template Construction 108
  - Range Input — /RI 108
  - Range Name — /RN 108
  - Range Name Table — /RNT 110
  - Worksheet Status — /WS 111
  - Spreadsheet Recalculation — /WGR 111
  - CALC Key — F9 113
  - Worksheet Global Defaults — /WGD 113
  - Printer Defaults 115
  - Other Defaults 117
  - Attach Add-In — /AA 119
  - Detach Add-In — /AD 121
  - Clear All Add-Ins — /AC 121
  - Attach an Add-In as Default Setting —
    /WGDOA 122
  - Invoke Add-In — /AI or ALT+F# 124
- GRAPHICS GENERAL INFORMATION 126
  - Graph Command 126
  - Graph Menu Selections 126
  - Current Graph 127
  - View — /GV 127
  - F10 (Graph) Key 127
  - Reset — /GR 128
- GRAPH CONSTRUCTION 129
  - BAR, STACKED-BAR, LINE Graph
    Construction 129
  - XY Graph Construction 130
  - PIE Chart Construction 131
  - Type — /GT 132
  - Group Data Range — /GG 132
- GRAPH OPTIONS 134
  - Grid — /GOG 134
  - Format Graph — /GOF 135
  - Data-labels — /GOD 136

Titles — /GOT 137
Legend — /GOL 138
Scale 139
Alter X or Y Scale — /GOSX or /GOSY 139
Scale Skip — /GOSS 141
Black and White or Color — /GOB or /GOC .. 142
Quit — /GOQ 142
GRAPH STORAGE 143
General Information 143
Save Graph — /GS 143
Name Graph — /GN 144
Difference Between Graph SAVE and
NAME 145
GRAPH PRINTING 147
PrintGraph Menu 147
PrintGraph Screen 148
Selecting and Cancelling Graphs to Print 149
Print Settings 149
Graph Size 150
Font 152
Eject 153
Pause 154
Range Colors 154
Change Graph/Font File Directories 155
Select Printer 156
Interface 157
Paper Size 157
Reset 158
Save Settings 159
MACRO GENERAL INFORMATION 160
Automatic Execution 160
Set Autoexec as a Default — /WGDA 160
Step Execution — ALT+F2 161
PLANNING AND CONSTRUCTING MACROS ... 163
Steps in Macro Construction 163
Placement of Macro Parts 163
Macro Label 164

Typing Macro Keystrokes	165
Function Keys used in Macros	166
Macro Annotation	167
Assigning a Macro Label — /RN	167
Run (Use) Macro — ALT+F3	169
MACRO LIBRARY MANAGER	170
General Information	170
Attach Library Manager Add-In — /AA	170
Detach Library Manager Add-In — /AD	172
Clear All Add-Ins — /AC	172
Attach Library Manager Add-In as Default Setting — /WGDOA	173
Invoke Library Manager Add-In — /AI or ALT+F#	175
Save Library File — /AIS	177
Edit Library File — /AIE	178
Load Library File — /AIL	180
Remove Library File — /AIR	181
List the Names of Macros in Current Library File — /AIN	181
LEARN	183
General Information	183
Specifying a Learn Range — /WLR	183
Recording Macro Keystrokes — ALT+F5	184
Cancel Learn Range — /WLC	185
Erase Contents of Learn Range — /WLE	185
/X MACRO COMMANDS	186
/X Commands	186
Advanced Macro Commands	187
LOOPING AND CALLING	190
Comparison of /XC, {subroutine}, /XG, {BRANCH}, and {DISPATCH}	190
{subroutine}	191
/XC (Call)	192
/XR or {RETURN}	193
{BRANCH}	193
/XG (GoTo)	193

{DISPATCH}	194
{DEFINE}	194
{ONERROR}	195
{RESTART}	195
{FOR}	196
{FORBREAK}	196
/XI or {IF}	197
{SYSTEM}	198
USER-DEFINED MACRO MENUS	199
\XM or {MENUBRANCH}	199
{MENUCALL}	200
Comparison of {MENUBRANCH} and {MENUCALL}	200
MACRO SUSPENSION	202
/XQ or {QUIT}	202
{BREAK}	202
{WAIT}	202
USER INPUT	203
The {?} Command	203
{GET}	203
/XL or {GETLABEL}	203
/XN or {GETNUMBER}	204
{LOOK}	205
SPREADSHEET MANIPULATION	206
{BLANK}	206
{CONTENTS}	206
{LET}	207
{PUT}	208
{RECALC}	208
{RECALCCOL}	209
CONTROLLING ENVIRONMENT	210
{BEEP}	210
{BORDERSOFF}/{BORDERSON} or {FRAMEOFF}/{FRAMEON}	210
{BREAKOFF}/{BREAKON}	210
{GRAPHOFF}/{GRAPHON}	210
{INDICATE}	211

CONTENTS

{PANELOFF}/{PANELON} 211
{WINDOWSOFF}/{WINDOWSON} 212
TEXT FILE MANIPULATION 213
   {OPEN} 213
   {CLOSE} 214
   {READ} 214
   {READLN} 214
   {WRITE} 215
   {WRITELN} 215
   {FILESIZE} 215
   {GETPOS} 216
   {SETPOS} 216
TIPS ABOUT MACROS 217
   Different Macros can Perform the
      Same Task 217
   Debugging Problem Macros 217
DATABASE GENERAL INFORMATION 220
   Database Terminology 220
   Setting up the Database 220
   The Data Command 221
   Data Menu Selections 221
DATA QUERIES 223
   Find Records — /DQF 223
   Extract Records — /DQE 225
   Extract Unique Records — /DQU 227
   Delete Records — /DQD 228
   Data Query Reset — /DQR 229
   Data Query Quit — /DQQ 230
   F7 (QUERY) Key 230
   Specifying Criteria 230
SORTING RECORDS 233
   General Information 233
   Data Sort Reset — /DSR 235
DATABASE STATISTICAL FUNCTIONS 236
MISCELLANEOUS DATA COMMANDS 238
   Data Fill — /DF 238
   Frequency Distribution — /DD 239

Create Data Table — /DT 239
Repeat Data Table — F8 241
Data Table Reset — /DTR 241
Data Matrix Invert — /DMI 244
Data Matrix Multiply — /DMM 244
Data Regression — /DR 245
Data Parse — /DP 247

Part IV   Index

PART I

Menus/Screens

	Page
Access System Menu	M-3
Worksheet Grid	M-4
/Worksheet Status Screen	M-5
/Worksheet Global Screen	M-6
/Worksheet Global Defaults Screen	M-7
/Print (Printer or File) Screen	M-8
/Graph Screen	M-9
Printgraph Menu	M-10

INTRODUCTION

This section contains a diagram of Access System Menu and the primary Screens that appear when Lotus is used.

ACCESS SYSTEM MENU

1-2-3 PrintGraph Translate Install Exit
Use 1-2-3

```
            1-2-3 Access System
           Copyright 1986, 1989
        Lotus Development Corporation
             All Rights Reserved
                 Release 2.2
```

The Access system lets you choose 1-2-3, PrintGraph, the Translate utility, and the Install program, from the menu at the top of this screen. If you're using a two-diskette system, the Access system may prompt you to change disks. Follow the instructions below to start a program.

o Use → or ← to move the menu pointer (the highlighted rectangle at the top of the screen) to the program you want to use.

o Press ENTER to start the program.

You can also start a program by typing the first character of its name.

Press HELP (F1) for more information.

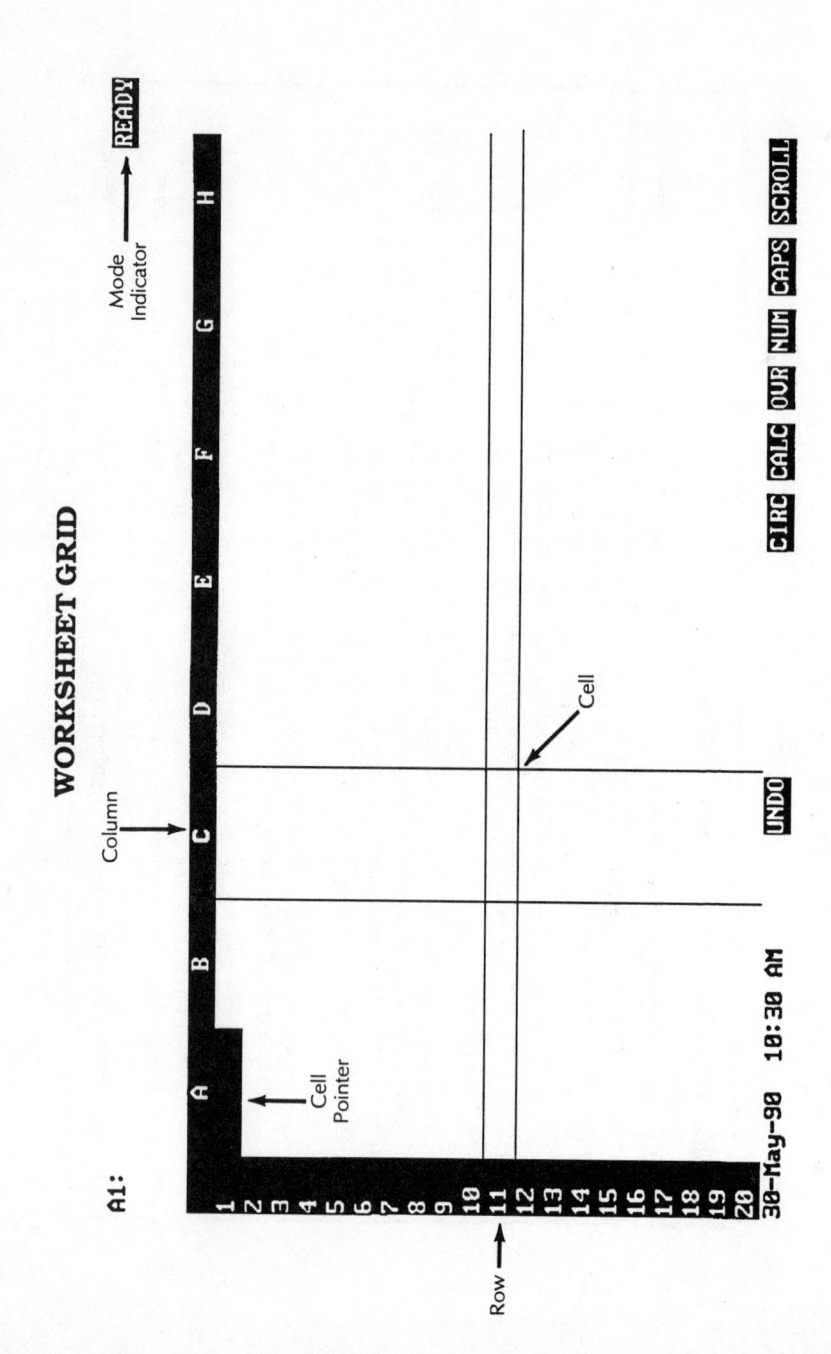

WORKSHEET GRID

Mode Indicator → **READY**

Column → **C**

Cell Pointer → (A1)

Cell

A1:

Columns: A B C D E F G H
Rows: 1–20

30-May-90 10:30 AM   **UNDO**   **CIRC CALC OUR NUM CAPS SCROLL**

Row

/WORKSHEET STATUS SCREEN

STAT

```
A1:
Press any key to continue...

                    ─────── Global Settings ───────
    Conventional memory:  165200 of 344480 Bytes (47%)
    Expanded memory:      (None)

    Math coprocessor:     (None)

    Recalculation:
      Method              Automatic
      Order               Natural
      Iterations          1

    Circular reference:   (None)

    Cell display:
      Format              (G)
      Label prefix        ' (left align)
      Column width        9
      Zero suppression    No

    Global protection:    Disabled

30-May-90  10:33 AM
```

/WORKSHEET GLOBAL SCREEN

A1:
Format Label-Prefix Column-Width Recalculation Protection Default Zero
Fixed Sci Currency , General +/- Percent Date Text Hidden   MENU

```
───────────────── Global Settings ─────────────────
Conventional memory:  165200 of 344480 Bytes (47%)
Expanded memory:      (None)

Math coprocessor:     (None)

Recalculation:
  Method              Automatic
  Order               Natural
  Iterations          1

Circular reference:   (None)

Cell display:
  Format              (G)
  Label prefix        ' (left align)
  Column width        9
  Zero suppression    No

Global protection:    Disabled
```

30-May-90 10:35 AM

MENUS/SCREENS

WORKSHEET GLOBAL DEFAULTS SCREEN

```
A1:
 Printer  Directory  Status  Update  Other  Autoexec  Quit
Specify printer interface and default settings
                    Default Settings
                    Directory: C:\123R2

Printer:
  Interface    Parallel 1           Autoexecute macros: Yes
  Auto linefeed  No
  Margins                           International:
    Left 4  Right 76  Top 2  Bottom 2    Punctuation      A
  Page length  66                       Decimal          Period
  Wait         No                       Argument         Comma
  Setup string                          Thousands        Comma
  Name         HP 2686 LaserJet Se...   Currency         Prefix: $
                                        Date format (D4) A (MM/DD/YY)
                                        Time format (D8) A (HH:MM:SS)
                                        Negative         Parentheses
Add-In:
  1                                 Help access method: Removable
  2                                 Clock display:      Standard
  3                                 Undo:               Enabled
  4                                 Beep:               Yes
  5
  6
  7
  8

30-May-90  10:37 AM
```

/PRINT (Printer or File) SCREEN

```
A1:
Range Line Page Options Clear Align Go Quit
Specify a range to print
                        ──── Print Settings ────
        Destination: Printer
        Range:

        Header:
        Footer:
        Margins:
           Left 4    Right 76   Top 2   Bottom 2
        Borders:
           Columns
           Rows
        Setup string:
        Page length: 66
        Output:      As-Displayed (Formatted)

30-May-90  10:42 AM
```

MENU

/GRAPH SCREEN

MENU

Type	X A B C D E F Reset View Save Options Name Group Quit
	Line Bar XY Stack-Bar Pie

```
┌─ Graph Settings ─────────────────────────────────────────────┐
│        Titles: First                                         │
│                Second                                        │
│                X axis                                        │
│                Y axis                                        │
│ Type: Line                                                   │
│                                                              │
│ X:                                                           │
│ A:                                                           │
│ B:                          Scaling    Y scale:   X scale:   │
│ C:                          Lower      Automatic  Automatic  │
│ D:                          Upper                            │
│ E:                          Format     (G)        (G)        │
│ F:                          Indicator  Yes        Yes        │
│                                                              │
│ Grid: None      Color: No                                    │
│                                                              │
│      Legend:         Format:   Data labels:       Skip: 1    │
│        A              Both                                   │
│        B              Both                                   │
│        C              Both                                   │
│        D              Both                                   │
│        E              Both                                   │
│        F              Both                                   │
└──────────────────────────────────────────────────────────────┘
```

30-May-90 10:43 AM

PRINTGRAPH MENU

Copyright 1986, 1989 Lotus Development Corp. All Rights Reserved. V2.2

Select graphs to print or preview
Image-Select Settings Go Align Page Exit   MENU

```
GRAPHS      IMAGE SETTINGS                        HARDWARE SETTINGS
TO PRINT    Size              Range colors        Graphs directory
              Top      .395      X                  A:\
              Left     .750      A                Fonts directory
              Width   6.500      B                  A:\
              Height  4.691      C                Interface
              Rotation .000      D                  Parallel 1
                                 E                Printer
                                 F
            Font                                  Paper size
              1 BLOCK1                              Width   8.500
              2 BLOCK1                              Length 11.000

                                                  ACTION SETTINGS
                                                    Pause No  Eject No
```

PART II

Commands

	Page
COMMAND LISTINGS GROUPED BY MENU	
Access System Menu Commands	C-3
1-2-3 Worksheet Commands (/W)	C-5
1-2-3 Range Commands (/R)	C-10
1-2-3 File Commands (/F)	C-12
1-2-3 Print Commands (/P)	C-14
1-2-3 Graph Commands (/G)	C-16
1-2-3 Data Commands (/D)	C-18
1-2-3 Add-In Commands (/A)	C-20

INTRODUCTION

This section contains an alphabetical listing of all Lotus commands. It also contains a page number on which further information about the command can be found.

ACCESS SYSTEM MENU COMMANDS

	Page
1-2-3	
/W (Worksheet)	C-5
/R (Range)	C-10
/C (Copy)	68
/M (Move)	70
/F (File)	C-12
/P (Print)	C-14
/G (Graph)	C-16
/D (Data)	C-18
/S (System)	11
/A (Add-in)	C-20
/Q (Quit)	11
PRINTGRAPH	147
IMAGE-SELECT	149
SETTINGS	149
Image	149
Size (Full, Half, Manual, Quit)	150
Font (1, 2)	152
Range-Colors	154
Hardware	149
Graphs-Directory	155
Fonts-Directory	155
Interface (1, 2, 3, 4, 5, 6, 7, 8)	157
Printer	156
Size-Paper (Length, Width, Quit)	157
Action	149
Pause	154
Eject	153
Save	159
Reset	158
GO	147
PAGE	147
EXIT	147

TRANSLATE 91
INSTALL . . . . *
EXIT 12

* Refer to the Lotus Manual that was supplied with your system.

1-2-3 WORKSHEET COMMANDS

/WG	WORKSHEET GLOBAL
/WGF	WORKSHEET GLOBAL Format 45
/WGFF	WORKSHEET GLOBAL Format Fixed 48
/WGFS	WORKSHEET GLOBAL Format Scientific 48
/WGFC	WORKSHEET GLOBAL Format Currency 49
/WGF,	WORKSHEET GLOBAL Format , 49
/WGFG	WORKSHEET GLOBAL Format General 50
/WGF+	WORKSHEET GLOBAL Format +/- 50
/WGFP	WORKSHEET GLOBAL Format Percent 50
/WGFD	WORKSHEET GLOBAL Format Date 51
/WGFD1	WORKSHEET GLOBAL Format Date 1 (DD-MMM-YY) 51
/WGFD2	WORKSHEET GLOBAL Format Date 2 (DD-MMM) 51
/WGFD3	WORKSHEET GLOBAL Format Date 3 (MMM-YY) 51
/WGFD4	WORKSHEET GLOBAL Format Date 4 (Long Intn'l) 51
/WGFD5	WORKSHEET GLOBAL Format Date 5 (Short Intn'l) 51
/WGFDT	WORKSHEET GLOBAL Format Date Time (selections 1 thru 4) 51
/WGFT	WORKSHEET GLOBAL Format Text 52
/WGFH	WORKSHEET GLOBAL Format Hidden 52
/WGL	WORKSHEET GLOBAL Label-Prefix 53
/WGLL	WORKSHEET GLOBAL Label-Prefix Left 53
/WGLR	WORKSHEET GLOBAL Label-Prefix Right 53
/WGLC	WORKSHEET GLOBAL Label-Prefix Center 53

/WGC	WORKSHEET GLOBAL Column Width	58
/WGR	WORKSHEET GLOBAL Recalculation	111
/WGRN	WORKSHEET GLOBAL Recalculation Natural	111
/WGRC	WORKSHEET GLOBAL Recalculation Columnwise	111
/WGRR	WORKSHEET GLOBAL Recalculation Rowwise	111
/WGRA	WORKSHEET GLOBAL Recalculation Automatic	111
/WGRM	WORKSHEET GLOBAL Recalculation Manual	111
/WGRI	WORKSHEET GLOBAL Recalculation Iteration	111
/WGP	WORKSHEET GLOBAL Protection	62
/WGPE	WORKSHEET GLOBAL Protection Enable	62
/WGPD	WORKSHEET GLOBAL Protection Disable	62
/WGD	WORKSHEET GLOBAL Default	62, 113
/WGDP	WORKSHEET GLOBAL Default Printer	113, 115
/WGDPI	WORKSHEET GLOBAL Default Printer Interface	113, 115
/WGDPA	WORKSHEET GLOBAL Default Printer AutoLF	113, 115
/WGDPL	WORKSHEET GLOBAL Default Printer Left	113, 115
/WGDPR	WORKSHEET GLOBAL Default Printer Right	113, 115
/WGDPT	WORKSHEET GLOBAL Default Printer Top	113, 115
/WGDPB	WORKSHEET GLOBAL Default Printer Bottom	113, 115

/WGDPP	WORKSHEET GLOBAL Default Printer Pg-Length 113, 115	
/WGDPS	WORKSHEET GLOBAL Default Printer Setup 113, 115	
/WGDPN	WORKSHEET GLOBAL Default Printer Name 113, 115	
/WGDD	WORKSHEET GLOBAL Default Directory	113
/WGDS	WORKSHEET GLOBAL Default Status	113
/WGDU	WORKSHEET GLOBAL Default Update	113
/WGDO	WORKSHEET GLOBAL Default Other 113, 117	
/WGDOI	WORKSHEET GLOBAL Default Other International 113, 117	
/WGDOIP	WORKSHEET GLOBAL Default Other International Punctuation (selections A through H) 113, 117	
/WGDOIC	WORKSHEET GLOBAL Default Other International Currency 113, 117	
/WGDOID	WORKSHEET GLOBAL Default Other International Date (selections A through D) 113, 117	
/WGDOIT	WORKSHEET GLOBAL Default Other International Time (selections A through D) 113, 117	
/WGDOIN	WORKSHEET GLOBAL Default Other International Negative (selections Parentheses, Sign) 113, 117	
/WGDOIQ	WORKSHEET GLOBAL Default Other International Quit 113, 117	
/WGDOH	WORKSHEET GLOBAL Default Other Help (selections Instant, Removable) 113, 117	
/WGDOC	WORKSHEET GLOBAL Default Other Clock (selections Standard, International, None, Clock, Filename) 113, 117	
/WGDOU	WORKSHEET GLOBAL Default Other Undo (selections Enable, Disable) 72, 113, 117	

/WGDOB	WORKSHEET GLOBAL Default Other Beep (selections Yes, No) 113, 117
/WGDOA	WORKSHEET GLOBAL Default Other Add-In (selections Set, Cancel) 113, 117, 122, 173
/WGDOQ	WORKSHEET GLOBAL Default Other Quit 113, 117
/WGDA	WORKSHEET GLOBAL Default Autoexec (selections Yes, No, Quit) 113, 160
/WGDQ	WORKSHEET GLOBAL Default Quit 113
/WGDZ	WORKSHEET GLOBAL Default Zero (selections No, Yes, Label) 113
/WI	WORKSHEET INSERT 67
/WIC	WORKSHEET INSERT Column 67
/WIR	WORKSHEET INSERT Row 67
/WD	WORKSHEET DELETE 65
/WDC	WORKSHEET DELETE Column 65
/WDR	WORKSHEET DELETE Row 65
/WC	WORKSHEET COLUMN
/WCS	WORKSHEET COLUMN Set-Width 56
/WCR	WORKSHEET COLUMN Reset-Width 56
/WCH	WORKSHEET COLUMN Hide 59
/WCD	WORKSHEET COLUMN Display 59
/WCC	WORKSHEET COLUMN Column-Range 57
/WCCS	WORKSHEET COLUMN Column-Range Set-Width 57
/WCCR	WORKSHEET COLUMN Column-Range Reset-Width 57
/WE	WORKSHEET ERASE (selections Yes, No) 64

1-2-3 WORKSHEET COMMANDS

/WT	WORKSHEET TITLES	60
/WTB	WORKSHEET TITLES Both	60
/WTH	WORKSHEET TITLES Horizontal	60
/WTV	WORKSHEET TITLES Vertical	60
/WTC	WORKSHEET TITLES Clear	60
/WW	WORKSHEET WINDOW	61
/WWH	WORKSHEET WINDOW Horizontal	61
/WWV	WORKSHEET WINDOW Vertical	61
/WWS	WORKSHEET WINDOW Sync	61
/WWU	WORKSHEET WINDOW Unsync	61
/WWC	WORKSHEET WINDOW Clear	61
/WS	WORKSHEET STATUS	111
/WP	WORKSHEET PAGE	101
/WL	WORKSHEET LEARN	183
/WLR	WORKSHEET LEARN Range	183
/WLC	WORKSHEET LEARN Cancel	185
/WLE	WORKSHEET LEARN Erase (selections Yes, No)	185

1-2-3 RANGE COMMANDS

/RF	RANGE FORMAT 46
/RFF	RANGE FORMAT Fixed 48
/RFS	RANGE FORMAT Scientific 48
/RFC	RANGE FORMAT Currency 49
/RF,	RANGE FORMAT , 49
/RFG	RANGE FORMAT General 50
/RF+	RANGE FORMAT +/- 50
/RFP	RANGE FORMAT Percent 50
/RFD	RANGE FORMAT Date 51
/RFD1	RANGE FORMAT Date 1 (DD-MMM-YY) 51
/RFD2	RANGE FORMAT Date 2 (DD-MMM) 51
/RFD3	RANGE FORMAT Date 3 (MMM-YY) 51
/RFD4	RANGE FORMAT Date 4 (Long Intn'l) 51
/RFD5	RANGE FORMAT Date 5 (Short Intn'l) 51
/RFDT	RANGE FORMAT Date Time (selections 1 through 4) 51
/RFT	RANGE FORMAT Date Text 52
/RFH	RANGE FORMAT Date Hidden 52
/RFR	RANGE FORMAT Date Reset 52
/RL	RANGE LABEL 52
/RLL	RANGE LABEL Left 52
/RLR	RANGE LABEL Right 52
/RLC	RANGE LABEL Center 52
/RE	RANGE ERASE 66
/RN	RANGE NAME 108
/RNC	RANGE NAME Create 108
/RND	RANGE NAME Delete 108

/RNL	RANGE NAME Label	108, 167
/RNLR	RANGE NAME Label Right	108
/RNLD	RANGE NAME Label Down	108
/RNLL	RANGE NAME Label Left	108
/RNLU	RANGE NAME Label Up	108
/RNR	RANGE NAME Reset	108
/RNT	RANGE NAME Table	110
/RJ	RANGE JUSTIFY	55
/RP	RANGE PROTECT	63
/RU	RANGE UNPROTECT	63
/RI	RANGE INPUT	108
/RV	RANGE VALUE	68
/RT	RANGE TRANSPOSE	69
/RS	RANGE SEARCH	73

1-2-3 FILE COMMANDS

/FR	FILE RETRIEVE	78
/FS	FILE SAVE	76
/FC	FILE COMBINE	79
/FCC	FILE COMBINE Copy	79
/FCA	FILE COMBINE Add	79
/FCS	FILE COMBINE Subtract	79
/FX	FILE XTRACT	81
/FXF	FILE XTRACT Formulas	81
/FXV	FILE XTRACT Values	81
/FE	FILE ERASE	84
/FEW	FILE ERASE Worksheet	84
/FEP	FILE ERASE Print	84
/FEG	FILE ERASE Graph	84
/FEO	FILE ERASE Other	84
/FL	FILE LIST	83
/FLW	FILE LIST Worksheet	83
/FLP	FILE LIST Print	83
/FLG	FILE LIST Graph	83
/FLO	FILE LIST Other	83
/FLL	FILE LIST Linked	83
/FI	FILE IMPORT	86
/FIT	FILE IMPORT Text	86
/FIN	FILE IMPORT Numbers	86
/FD	FILE DIRECTORY	83

/FA	FILE ADMIN	
/FAR	FILE ADMIN Reservation	89
/FAT	FILE ADMIN Table	87
/FAL	FILE ADMIN Link-Refresh	89

1-2-3 PRINT COMMANDS

/PP	PRINT PRINTER/FILE	94
/PPR	PRINT PRINTER/FILE Range	95
/PPL	PRINT PRINTER/FILE Line	95
/PPP	PRINT PRINTER/FILE Page	95
/PPO	PRINT PRINTER/FILE Options	95
/PPOH	PRINT PRINTER/FILE Options Header	101
/PPOF	PRINT PRINTER/FILE Options Footer	101
/PPOM	PRINT PRINTER/FILE Options Margins	97
/PPOML	PRINT PRINTER/FILE Options Margins Left	97
/PPOMR	PRINT PRINTER/FILE Options Margins Right	97
/PPOMT	PRINT PRINTER/FILE Options Margins Top	99
/PPOMB	PRINT PRINTER/FILE Options Margins Bottom	99
/PPOMN	PRINT PRINTER/FILE Options Margins None	105
/PPOB	PRINT PRINTER/FILE Options Borders	95–96
/PPOBC	PRINT PRINTER/FILE Options Border Columns	95–96
/PPOBR	PRINT PRINTER/FILE Options Border Rows	95–96
/PPOS	PRINT PRINTER/FILE Options Setup	103
/PPOP	PRINT PRINTER/FILE Options Pg-Length	100
/PPOO	PRINT PRINTER/FILE Options Other	95–96

1-2-3 PRINT COMMANDS

/PPOOA   PRINT PRINTER/FILE Options Other
              As-Displayed   95–96

/PPOOC   PRINT PRINTER/FILE Options Other
              Cell-Formulas   95–96

/PPOOF   PRINT PRINTER/FILE Options Other
              Formatted   95–96

/PPOOU   PRINT PRINTER/FILE Options Other
              Unformatted   95–96

/PPOQ   PRINT PRINTER/FILE Options Quit   95–96

/PPC   PRINT PRINTER/FILE Clear   104
/PPCA   PRINT PRINTER/FILE Clear All   104
/PPCR   PRINT PRINTER/FILE Clear Range   104
/PPCB   PRINT PRINTER/FILE Clear Borders   104
/PPCF   PRINT PRINTER/FILE Clear Format   104

/PPA   PRINT PRINTER/FILE Align   95

/PPG   PRINT PRINTER/FILE Go   95

/PPQ   PRINT PRINTER/FILE Quit   95

1-2-3 GRAPH COMMANDS

/GT	GRAPH TYPE	132
/GTL	GRAPH TYPE Line	129
/GTB	GRAPH TYPE Bar	129
/GTX	GRAPH TYPE XY	130
/GTS	GRAPH TYPE Stack-Bar	129
/GTP	GRAPH TYPE Pie	131
/GX	GRAPH X-AXIS	129, 130, 131
/GA	GRAPH A-AXIS	129, 130, 131
/GB	GRAPH B-AXIS	129, 130
/GC	GRAPH C-AXIS	129, 130
/GD	GRAPH D-AXIS	129, 130
/GE	GRAPH E-AXIS	129, 130
/GF	GRAPH F-AXIS	129, 130
/GR	GRAPH RESET	128
/GRG	GRAPH RESET Graph	128
/GRX	GRAPH RESET X	128
/GRA	GRAPH RESET A	128
/GRB	GRAPH RESET B	128
/GRC	GRAPH RESET C	128
/GRD	GRAPH RESET D	128
/GRE	GRAPH RESET E	128
/GRF	GRAPH RESET F	128
/GRR	GRAPH RESET Ranges	128

/GRO	GRAPH RESET Options	128
/GRQ	GRAPH RESET Quit	128
/GV	GRAPH VIEW	127
/GS	GRAPH SAVE	143
/GO	GRAPH OPTIONS	134
/GOL	GRAPH OPTIONS Legend (selections A through F and Range)	138
/GOF	GRAPH OPTIONS Format (selections Graph, A through F, and Quit)	135
/GOT	GRAPH OPTIONS Titles (selections First, Second, X-Axis, and Y-Axis)	137
/GOG	GRAPH OPTIONS Grid (selections Horizontal, Vertical, Both, Clear)	134
/GOS	GRAPH OPTIONS Scale (selections Y-Scale, X-Scale, Skip)	139, 141
/GOC	GRAPH OPTIONS Color	142
/GOB	GRAPH OPTIONS B&W	142
/GOD	GRAPH OPTIONS Data-Labels (selections A through F, Group and Quit)	136
/GOQ	GRAPH OPTIONS Quit	142
/GN	GRAPH NAME	144
/GNU	GRAPH NAME Use	144
/GNC	GRAPH NAME Create	144
/GND	GRAPH NAME Delete	144
/GNR	GRAPH NAME Reset	144
/GNT	GRAPH NAME Table	144
/GG	GRAPH GROUP	132
/GQ	GRAPH QUIT	126

1-2-3 DATA COMMANDS

/DF	DATA FILL 238
/DT	DATA TABLE 239
/DT1	DATA TABLE 1 239
/DT2	DATA TABLE 2 239
/DTR	DATA TABLE Reset 241
/DS	DATA SORT 233
/DSD	DATA SORT Data-Range 233
/DSP	DATA SORT Primary-Key 233
/DSS	DATA SORT Secondary-Key 233
/DSR	DATA SORT Reset 235
/DSG	DATA SORT Go 233
/DSQ	DATA SORT Quit 233
/DQ	DATA QUERY 223
/DQI	DATA QUERY Input 223, 225, 228
/DQC	DATA QUERY Criteria 223, 225, 228
/DQO	DATA QUERY Output 225
/DQF	DATA QUERY Find 223
/DQE	DATA QUERY Extract 225
/DQU	DATA QUERY Unique 227
/DQD	DATA QUERY Delete (selections Cancel, Delete) 228
/DQR	DATA QUERY Reset 229
/DQQ	DATA QUERY Quit 230
/DD	DATA DISTRIBUTION 239

/DM	DATA MATRIX	244
/DMI	DATA MATRIX Invert	244
/DMM	DATA MATRIX Multiply	244
/DR	DATA REGRESSION	245
/DRX	DATA REGRESSION X-Range	245
/DRY	DATA REGRESSION Y-Range	245
/DRO	DATA REGRESSION Output-Range	245
/DRI	DATA REGRESSION Intercept - selections Compute, Zero	245
/DRR	DATA REGRESSION Reset	245
/DRG	DATA REGRESSION Go	245
/DRQ	DATA REGRESSION Quit	245
/DP	DATA PARSE	247
/DPF	DATA PARSE Format-Line (selections Create, Edit)	247
/DPI	DATA PARSE Input-Column	247
/DPO	DATA PARSE Output-Range	247
/DPR	DATA PARSE Reset	247
/DPG	DATA PARSE Go	247
/DPQ	DATA PARSE Quit	247

1-2-3 ADD-IN COMMANDS

/AA   ADD-IN ATTACH   119, 170

/AD   ADD-IN DETACH   121, 172

/AI   ADD-IN INVOKE   124, 175

/AC   ADD-IN CLEAR   121, 172

1-2-3 MISCELLANEOUS COMMANDS

/C   COPY   68

/M   MOVE   70

/S   SYSTEM   11

/Q   QUIT   11

PART III

Reference Guide

Detailed instructions on the operation of each aspect of Lotus 1-2-3 are contained in this section.

	Page #
General Information	3
System Start-up	9
Screen Orientation	13
Input	19
Built-In Functions	28
Formatting	45
Editing	64
Storage	76
Translate Files	91
Printing	94
Miscellaneous	108
Graphics General Information	126
Graph Construction	129
Graph Options	134
Graph Storage	143
Graph Printing	147
Macro General Information	160
Planning/Constructing Macros	163
Macro Library Manager	170

Learn	183
Macro Commands	186
Looping and Calling Macros	190
User-Defined Macro Menus	199
Marco Suspension	202
User Input	203
Spreadsheet Manipulation	206
Controlling Environment	210
Text File Manipulation	213
Tips About Macros	217
Sample Database	218
Database General Information	220
Data Queries	223
Sorting Records	233
Database Statistical Functions	236
Miscellaneous Data Commands	238

GENERAL INFORMATION

Menus

The Lotus system is a very powerful software package. It is relatively easy to operate. The system is set up with a series of two-line menus, the first of which appears whenever the **SLASH** key is pressed.

NOTE: The exception to this is the Access System Menu that appears after system start-up or whenever you Quit 1-2-3 (see page 11).

The top line of each menu gives you a listing of all available choices. This line also contains a pointer that can be moved to highlight (point to) the desired menu selection (see below).

The second line of each menu contains more information about the menu selection over which the pointer is located.

Selections are made from menus in one of two ways:

- Use the directional arrows to position the pointer over the desired menu choice.
- Press the **ENTER** key.

OR

- Type the first letter of the desired menu choice.

Command Structure

All commands are given to Lotus in basically the same way:

1. Press the SLASH (/) key.

2. Make choices from the menu(s) which appear.

   Either:
   - Press the **Left** or **Right** Directional **Arrow** Key to position the pointer over the desired command choice then press the **ENTER** key.

     OR
   - Type the first letter of the desired menu choice.

3. Follow any messages that appear on the screen:
   - If another menu appears, follow Step 2 above.
   - If the system prompts for a filename, a range name, or a number, type the name or number then press **ENTER**.
   - If the system prompts you to specify a range, point to or type the range then press **ENTER**. For more information on specifying a range, see below.

Specifying a Range

Many commands require that you specify the range of cells that will be affected by the command.

When specifying the range, you need only specify the first (upper left) and last (lower right) cell in the range.

EXAMPLE: The range A1..C3 (A1 through C3) would include the following cells:

A1	B1	C1
A2	B2	C2
A3	B3	C3

To specify a range, you can either *type* the range coordinates or *point to* the range.

To TYPE the range coordinates:

1. Type the first coordinate (upper left cell in the range).
2. Press the **PERIOD** key.
3. Type the last coordinate (lower right cell in the range).

To POINT TO the range:

1. Move the pointer to the first cell in the range.
2. Press the **PERIOD** key.

   NOTE: In some commands the pointer is positioned over the first cell in the range *before* the command is given. If this is the case, omit Steps 1 and 2 above.

3. Move the pointer to the last cell in the range.

   The entire range of cells will appear highlighted.

Name—F3

The Name key (**F3**) can be used to display a list of range names or filenames. When **F3** is pressed the following will occur:

- If **F3** is pressed whenever a command causes a list of range names or filenames to appear in the Control Panel, the system will display an entire screenload of those names. During some commands, additional information will also appear whenever the cursor is located on one of those names.

  EXAMPLE: The **/Range N**ame **L**abel **C**reate command (page 108) will display the first five assigned range names. When you press **F3**, a maximum of 105 assigned range names will appear. Whenever the cursor is positioned over one of those range names, the coordinates of the range will appear.

EXAMPLE: The **/F**ile **R**etrieve command (page 78) will display the first five available filenames. When you press **F3**, a maximum of 105 available filenames will appear. Whenever the cursor is positioned over one of those filenames, the DOS date, time, and size (in bytes) of that file will appear.

- If **F3** is pressed whenever the system is in the POINT mode, the system will display the first five available range names. If **F3** is pressed again, a maximum of 105 available range names will appear. Whenever the cursor is positioned over one of those range names, the coordinates of the range will appear.

- If **F3** is pressed during formula construction, the system will display the first five available range names. If **F3** is pressed again, a maximum of 105 available range names will appear. Whenever the cursor is positioned over one of those range names, the coordinates of the range will appear.

ESC Key

The **ESC** key has two purposes:

- To cancel the input of an entry. **ESC** must be pressed before the entry is accepted onto the worksheet.

- To "back out" of any command. Each time **ESC** is pressed, the system will back up to the previous menu or step in the command.

Help — F1

The Lotus program is equipped with an on-line Help feature. This feature will display Help information on the screen whenever the **F1** key is pressed.

GENERAL INFORMATION

1. To view a HELP screen, press the **F1** key.

   The information that appears directly relates to the current command, function, activity, or mode.

   Several highlighted topics will appear on each screen. Information about any of these topics can be viewed by moving the pointer to the desired topic and pressing the **ENTER** key. To move the pointer:

Key:	Moves pointer to:
Left Arrow	Previous topic
Right Arrow	Next topic
Home	First topic
End	Last topic

   You can view an index of Help screens by moving the pointer to the *Help Index* topic and pressing the **ENTER** key.

2. To clear a Help screen, press the **ESC** key.

Disk Handling

Disks must be handled carefully. There are several things which you must remember when handling disks:

- Never touch the exposed areas of the disk.
- Never expose a disk to any magnetic field.
- Do not bend or fold a disk.
- Do not expose the disk to any extreme heat or cold.
- Do not drop any liquid, food, or ashes on the disk.
- When the disk is not in use, keep it stored in its protective outer envelope.

Any of the above could damage the disk and make it impossible to read information from or write information to the disk.

Write-Protect

There is a small "notch" on the upper right side of the disk. When this notch is covered with one of the "write-protect tabs" that are supplied with each box of blank disks, the disk is write-protected.

No information can be written to (recorded on) a write-protected disk. Write-protecting a disk is a good way to prevent accidental revisions or erasures.

Whenever the write-protect tab is removed from the notch, information can again be recorded onto the disk.

SYSTEM STARTUP

Each computer starts Lotus a bit differently. If you have any difficulty with the steps outlined below, consult either the computer's operations manual or the Lotus manual for that computer system.

Installation

The Lotus 1-2-3 program must be installed properly. For detailed information on installation (or uninstallation), see the Lotus manual that was supplied with your system.

System Startup

To start Lotus:

1. Carefully remove the Lotus system disk from its protective outer envelope and insert it into disk drive A. Close the disk drive door.

   NOTE: If you are working on a hard disk system with Lotus resident on the disk, disregard Step 1.

2. If the system has a separate monitor, turn the monitor power ON.

3. Turn the computer power ON.

4. If necessary, enter the current date and time. After typing each, press **ENTER**.

5. When the operating system prompt appears on your screen:

   a. Be sure the Lotus System Disk #1 is inserted in disk drive A.

      NOTE: If you are working on a hard disk system with Lotus resident on the disk, disregard Step 5a. Instead use the **CD** command to

CHANGE to the sub-DIRECTORY which contains the LOTUS.COM file.

b. Type the letters LOTUS.

c. Press **ENTER**.

The Lotus Access System Menu will appear on your screen.

Lotus Access System Menu

A menu that appears in a program is a list of commands that can be given to the system. The Lotus Access System Menu is the first menu that appears after the system has been started.

- The FIRST LINE of the menu contains the available choices: "1-2-3, PrintGraph, Translate, Install, Exit."

- The brightened square (POINTER) is HIGHLIGHTING (pointing to) the first choice "(1-2-3)."

- The SECOND LINE of the menu contains more information about what that particular choice means ("Use 1-2-3, Print 1-2-3 graphs, Transfer data between 1-2-3 and other programs, Install 1-2-3, Return to operating system").

- To make a selection from this menu (or any menu):
  - Press one of the **ARROW** keys to move the pointer to the desired choice and press **ENTER**.

    OR

  - Type the first letter of the desired menu choice.

- To begin using Lotus for Spreadsheet construction, edit or print:

    1. Make sure the pointer is located over 1-2-3.

    2. Press **ENTER**.

       The Lotus Copyright Screen will appear

SYSTEM STARTUP 11

briefly. When it clears, the blank worksheet grid will appear. See pages 13–16 for an explanation of the elements of the grid.

Quit 1-2-3 — /Q

The QUIT command will end the current 1-2-3 session and return the system to the Lotus Access System Menu. Any worksheet that is not saved before the QUIT command is given will be lost.

1. Press the SLASH (/) key.

   The Main Menu will appear.

2. Type Q to select Quit.

   A verification menu will appear.

3. Either:
   - Type Y to select Yes (Quit 1-2-3), or
   - Type N to select No (cancel the Quit command)

   NOTE: To temporarily exit to the operating system without losing the spreadsheet information on the screen, see below.

Temporarily Exit to Operating System — /S

The SYSTEM command will allow you to exit to the operating system without ending the current 1-2-3 session. Any worksheet that is not saved before the command is given will NOT be lost. It will remain in the system memory and will return to the screen when you return to 1-2-3.

To temporarily exit to the operating system:

1. Press the SLASH (/) key.

   The Main Menu will appear.

2. Type **S** to select **S**ystem.

    The operating system prompt will appear. While this prompt is on the screen, most DOS commands (such as DIR, COPY, DEL, and so on) can be executed. To return to 1-2-3:

3. Type **EXIT** and press **ENTER**.

    1-2-3 will return to your screen.

    NOTE: To exit 1-2-3 and return to the Access System Menu or the operating system prompt, see below.

Exit System — E

The EXIT SYSTEM command will allow you to exit from Lotus and return to the operating system.

The Lotus Access System Menu must be on the screen before the command can be given.

Type **E** to select **E**xit.

The operating system prompt will appear.

SCREEN ORIENTATION

Control Panel

The very top of the screen (above the letters A through H) is known as the CONTROL PANEL. Menus, prompts, and other important information will appear in this area.

- The CELL ADDRESS appears in the upper left corner of the screen. This confirms that the cell pointer is resting on a specific cell address. As the cell pointer moves around on the screen, the current CELL ADDRESS will always appear in this area.

  The CONTENTS of a cell will appear next to the CELL ADDRESS whenever the pointer is located over that cell, along with the cell's format (see page 46), any column width setting (pages 56–57) and range protection status (page 63).

- The upper right corner of the screen contains the MODE INDICATOR. This indicator changes as the system changes modes:

  READY The system is ready to accept a command or cell input.

  MENU A menu is currently on the screen.

  FILES A list of filenames is currently on the screen.

  NAMES A list of range, graph, or available add-in names is currently on the screen.

  EDIT You are currently editing the contents of a cell.

  POINT You are using the pointer to specify a range of cells to be affected by a command.

  FIND A Data Query Find operation is being executed (see page 223).

LABEL The text being typed is a label.

VALUE The information being typed is a value or formula.

HELP A Help screen is being displayed.

STATUS A screen appears displaying worksheet status (/WS command on page 111, /WGDS command on page 113).

ERROR An error has occurred.

WAIT The system is performing a calculation or completing a command.

FRMT A format line is being edited with Data Parse (see page 247).

- The CELL POINTER is moved to different cells by using the DIRECTIONAL ARROW and POINTER MOVEMENT KEYS located on the right side of the keyboard. See page 16 for a list of all keys that can be used to move the pointer.

- LOCK INDICATORS and OTHER INDICATORS frequently appear on the bottom line of the screen.

    CALC The system is set for manual recalculation. The indicator is telling you that it is necessary to press the **F9** key for the sheet to display properly recalculated figures. See page 111 for information on manual and automatic recalculation.

    CAPS The keyboard is locked into upper case (capitals); all letters typed will appear as capitals. The **CAPS LOCK** key will lock and unlock CAPS.

    CIRC Appears whenever a circular reference appears on the worksheet.

    CMD Appears when the system pauses during macro execution.

    END Appears whenever the **END** key is pressed.

    MEM The memory is 4000 bytes away from becoming full.

SCREEN ORIENTATION

NUM The system is locked into numerics; the numeric keypad can be used to type numbers instead of move the pointer. The **NUM LOCK** key will lock and unlock numerics.

OVR The **INS** key toggles the system between insert and overstrike mode. The OVR indicator appears whenever the system is locked into overstrike.

SCROLL SCROLL is locked on (see page 16).

SST The system has paused for operator input during step execution of a macro.

STEP The system is processing step execution of a macro (see page 161).

UNDO Undo mode is set on (see page 72).

Worksheet Grid

The main portion of the screen is taken up by the worksheet "grid." All numbers, formulas, and text are typed onto this grid.

- Horizontal ROWS on the grid are numbered. The row numbers appear at the extreme left of the screen.

- Vertical COLUMNS on the grid are lettered. The column letters appear across the top of the screen.

- The intersection of a row and a column is called a CELL. A CELL is the location where each number or label is typed on the worksheet.

- The cell is identified by the column letter and row number that intersect to form it. This is called the CELL ADDRESS. For example, the intersection of column A and row 1 is CELL ADDRESS A1. The intersection of column C and row 10 is CELL ADDRESS C10.

- The brightened area that appears within the worksheet grid is called the CELL POINTER. The CELL POINTER POINTS to the cell that is currently active. Whenever a label, value or formula is typed, it appears in the cell over which the pointer is located.

Scrolling

The screen is a "window" that displays only a portion of the worksheet at any given time. The screen window can be moved (scrolled) so that other parts of the worksheet can be viewed. This will happen whenever one of the cell pointer movement keys below is used to move the pointer to a cell outside the current window.

The **SCROLL LOCK** key is used to lock the scroll feature on and off. When the scroll lock feature is on, the directional arrow keys will cause the worksheet to scroll through the available screen space.

NOTE: The SCROLL indicator will appear on the screen whenever the scroll lock feature is on (see page 15).

Cell Pointer Movement

Key:	Moves cell pointer:
ARROW Keys	one cell in the direction indicated on the keycap
HOME	directly to cell A1, the HOME position
END+HOME	to the extreme lower right boundaries of the worksheet
END+RIGHT ARROW	right to first intersection of blank and non-blank cell

SCREEN ORIENTATION

END+LEFT ARROW left to first intersection of blank and non-blank cell

END+UP ARROW up to first intersection of blank and non-blank cell

END+DOWN ARROW down to first intersection of blank and non-blank cell

PG DN one screenload (page) down

PG UP one screenload (page) up

TAB, CTRL+RIGHT ARROW one screenload (page) to the right

SHIFT+TAB, CTRL + LEFT ARROW one screenload (page) to the left

Function Keys

Function keys perform the following tasks:

Key:	Function:	See Page
F1	Help	6
F2	Edit	19
F3	Name	5
F4	Abs	26
F5	GoTo	18
F6	Window	61
F7	Query	230
F8	Table	241
F9	Calc	113
F10	Graph	127
Alt+F1	Compose	23
Alt+F2	Step	161
Alt+F3	Run	164
Alt+F4	Undo	72
Alt+F5	Learn	184
Alt+F7 through **Alt+F10**	Invokes Add-ins	119

GoTo — F5

The **F5** key can be used to GO TO any specified cell.

1. Press **F5**.

   The message "Enter address to go to" will appear in the control panel.

2. Type the coordinate of the cell to go to.

   The characters will appear as you type them.

3. Press **ENTER**.

   The cell pointer will move directly to the cell.

Range Search — /RS

The **R**ange **S**earch command will search through a specified range for a specified character string. See page 73 for information on using this command.

INPUT

Typing Information on the Worksheet

All information is typed on the worksheet in basically the same way:

1. Position the pointer over the cell where the information is to appear.

2. Type the information:

   LABEL Any text that is typed into the worksheet and is not used for calculation (see page 20).

   VALUE Any number that is directly typed onto a worksheet (see page 24).

   FORMULA Any numeric formula that is typed. When a formula is typed, the *results* of the formula appear on the sheet, although the system remembers the formula itself. These results will change whenever other cells which the formula references change (see page 24).

3. Press **ENTER** or one of the **Arrow** keys to accept the information onto the worksheet.

   When **ENTER** is pressed, the pointer remains over the cell where the information appears. When one of the **Arrow** keys is pressed, the pointer will move one cell in the direction of the arrow.

Error Correction

If you make an error *while* typing information:

1. Press the **BACKSPACE** key enough times to erase the incorrect character(s).

2. Type the correct character(s).

If you make an error *after* accepting information onto the worksheet:

1. Position the cell pointer over the cell that contains the incorrect information.
2. Press the **F2** (Edit) key.

   The contents of the cell will appear on the *edit line* and the mode indicator will change to EDIT.
3. Edit the label:
   - The **Left** and **Right Arrow** keys will move the edit line pointer.
   - The **BACKSPACE** key will backspace and delete characters.
   - The **DEL** key will delete characters at the edit line pointer location.
   - All characters typed will be inserted at the edit line pointer location unless you press the **INS** key to toggle to overstrike mode.
4. Press **ENTER**.

Typing Labels

A LABEL is any text that is typed into the worksheet and is not used for calculation.

When typing a label, the first character typed MUST be an alphabetical character or one of the label prefixes (see page 21).

To type a label:

1. Position the pointer over the cell where label is to appear.
2. Type the label prefix (if necessary).
3. Type the label.

NOTE: To produce a capital letter, hold **SHIFT** and type the letter. To lock in or out of upper case, press the **CAPS LOCK** key.

4. Press **ENTER** or one of the **Arrow** keys to accept the label onto the worksheet.

When **ENTER** is pressed, the pointer remains over the cell where the information appears. When one of the **Arrow** keys is pressed, the pointer will move one cell in the direction of the arrow.

NOTE: Labels which are longer than the width of the column will fill adjacent unoccupied columns. If the adjacent column is occupied, the label will appear truncated. To change the width of a column, see page 56 or 58.

Label Prefixes

When labels are typed and accepted onto the worksheet, two things happen:

- The label automatically aligns with the left side of the column,
- The label prefix for left-justify (') appears before the label in the control panel whenever the pointer rests on the cell containing that label.

Left-justify is the default label prefix. The default label prefix can be changed by using the Global Label-prefix command (see page 53).

Individual labels can be left-justified, right-justified, or centered by typing the appropriate label prefix as the first character during input.

These label prefixes are:

    '   left-justify
    "   right-justify
    ^   center

Individual labels can be edited to appear left-justified or right-justified or centered by deleting the existing label prefix and inserting the desired label prefix (see "Error Correction," page 19)

A range of labels can be changed to left-justified, right-justified, or centered by using the Range Label Prefix command (page 52).

NOTE: Two additional label prefixes are available:

    /   A slash produces a repeating label (see below).

    | A vertical produces a nonprinting note. The contents of a cell with this label prefix, as well as all subsequent cells in that row, will appear on the screen but will not be printed.

Repeating Label

A repeating label is a character that repeats throughout the width of a column.

1. Position the pointer over the cell in which the repeating label is to appear.

2. Press the **BACKSLASH** key once.

3. Type the character that you want to fill the cell. This character should be typed only ONCE.

4. Press **ENTER** or one of the **Arrow** keys to accept the repeating label onto the worksheet.

    When **ENTER** is pressed, the pointer remains over the cell where the information appears. When one of the **Arrow** keys is pressed, the pointer will move one cell in the direction of the arrow.

INPUT

Compose — ALT+F1

The Compose keys (**ALT+F1**) can be used to construct many characters that are not available on a standard keyboard. To use compose:

1. Position the pointer over the cell in which the composed character or symbol is to appear.

    NOTE: The system must be in either the READY, LABEL, or EDIT mode before compose can be used.

2. Hold **ALT** and press **F1**.

    NOTE: No prompts or messages will appear on the screen after these keys are pressed.

3. Type the *character sequence* that corresponds with the desired character.

    The character sequence will not appear as it is typed; however, the character itself will appear as soon as the sequence is complete.

    EXAMPLE: The *character sequence* for the British pound sterling sign (**£**) is the letter **L** and the equal sign **=**. Therefore, to create the pound sign, press **ALT+F1**, then type **L=**. The pound sign will appear.

    NOTE: For a list of all available characters and corresponding character sequences, refer to the Lotus manual that was supplied with your system.

4. Press **ENTER** or one of the **Arrow** keys to accept the character onto the worksheet.

    NOTE: Additional characters may be typed into the cell before **ENTER** is pressed in Step 4 above.

NOTE: Any listed Lotus International Character Set (LICS) characters can be created with the compose key. However, some monitors may not be able to display all characters and some printers may not be able to print all characters.

Typing Values

A value is any number that is directly typed onto a worksheet. To type a value:

1. Position the pointer over the cell in which the value is to appear.
2. Type the value.
3. Press **ENTER** or one of the **Arrow** keys to accept the value onto the worksheet.

   When **ENTER** is pressed, the pointer remains over the cell where the information appears. When one of the **Arrow** keys is pressed, the pointer will move one cell in the direction of the arrow.

   NOTE: If a value contains more digits than will fit in the column, the value will appear in exponential notation. If the exponential notation will not fit in the column, a line of asterisks will appear. If the cell containing the value has a range format and the value will not fit in the column, a line of asterisks will appear. To change the width of the column, see pages 56–58.

Typing Formulas

When a formula is typed and accepted into a cell, the *results* of the formula appear on the worksheet. However, the system remembers the formula itself. These results will change whenever other cells that the formula references change.

INPUT

There are four types of formulas:

Numeric — calculates numbers;
String — joins character strings;
Logical — returns a logical true or false; and
@functions — built in functions (see page 28).

To type any of these formulas:

1. Position the pointer over the cell in which the formulas is to appear.

2. Type the formula. The first character typed must be one of the following:

    + - (. @ $ any number

    NOTE: The following keys can be used as operators:

+	add	−	subtract
/	divide	×	multiply
^	exponential		
=	equals	<>	not equal to
<	less than	>	greater than
	or equal to	=	or equal to
#OR#	logical or	**#NOT#**	logical not
#AND#	logical and	&	string concatenation

3. Press **ENTER** or one of the **Arrow** keys to accept the formula onto the worksheet.

    When **ENTER** is pressed, the pointer remains over the cell where the information appears. When one of the **Arrow** keys is pressed, the pointer will move one cell in the direction of the arrow.

    NOTE: If the result of a formula contains more digits than will fit in the column, the value will appear in exponential notation. If the exponential notation will not fit in the column, a line of asterisks will appear. If the cell containing the formula has a range format and the result of the formula will not fit in the column, a line of asterisks will appear. To change the width of the column, see pages 56–58.

Absolute Values

Whenever a formula is copied or moved to a new location on the worksheet, the parts of the formula are automatically adjusted relative to their new position.

EXAMPLE: The formula (A1/B1) is located in cell C1. When the formula is copied to cells C2 and C3, the copied formula automatically adjusts to its new positions.

	A	B	C
Row 1	100	200	(A1/B1)
Row 2	200	300	(A2/B2)
Row 3	300	400	(A3/B3)

If you do not want one or more parts of the formula to adjust, you must tell the system that these parts are ABSOLUTE VALUES. The dollar sign symbol tells the system *not* to adjust this part of the formula relative to its new position during a MOVE or COPY operation. It signifies ABSOLUTE VALUE.

EXAMPLE: When the formula in cell C1 (A1/B$1) is copied to rows 2 and 3, the row coordinate in the second part of the formula is not adjusted relative to position. This part of the formula is *absolute* and is always copied "as is."

	A	B	C
Row 1	100	200	(A1/B$1)
Row 2	200	300	(A2/B$1)
Row 3	300	400	(A3/B$1)

Although the FIRST part of the formula was adjusted (A1 in the original formula, A2 in the row 2 copy of the formula, A3 in the row 3 copy of the formula), the second part of the formula remained the same (B$1).

The dollar sign may be typed when the formula is typed (page 24), or may be added during formula editing (page 19). The **F4** (Abs) key can be used to insert the dollar sign into a formula. To use **F4**, position the cursor over the portion of the formula to be made absolute. For example, position the cursor over either the A or the 1 in the formula (A1+B1). The first time **F4** is pressed, dollar signs will be added to both the row and column portion of the address (A1). The second time **F4** is pressed, the dollar sign will appear before only the row (A$1). The third time, the dollar sign appears in only the column ($A1). The fourth time **F4** is pressed, all dollar signs will disappear (A1).

NOTE: See page 68 or 70 for information on the MOVE and COPY commands.

SUM Formula Construction

Functions which are performed repeatedly are stored within Lotus. These are called BUILT-IN FUNCTIONS. The @SUM built-in formula will produce a total (or sum) of all cells within a given range. To construct a SUM formula:

1. Position the pointer over the cell in which the SUM formula is to appear.
2. Type the symbol **@** .
3. Type the FUNCTION NAME (in this case, **SUM**).
4. Type the range of cells to be affected within parentheses.

   EXAMPLE: @SUM(B14..B22).

   NOTE: When typing the range of cells, include any blank cell before the first cell in the range to be added and after the last cell in the range to be added. This will allow you to delete the first or last cell in the range without producing ERR messages.

   EXAMPLE: Instead of typing @SUM(B15..B21), type @SUM(B14..B22).

   NOTE: See pages 28–44 for additional built-in functions.

BUILT-IN FUNCTIONS

Date and Time Functions

The Date and Time Functions store dates and times in a way that allows you to perform calculations on those dates and times.

NOTE: The functions below will produce a number that represents the date or time. Use the date and time format commands (pages 45 and 51) to format these numbers to appear as dates or times.

The following is a list of date and time functions:

Date Functions

@DATE(year,month,day)
 display the date for the specified year, month and day.

 EXAMPLE: @DATE(90,2,25) will produce a number that represents the date February 25, 1990.

@DAY(date-number)
@MONTH(date-number)
@YEAR(date-number)
 @DAY will display the number of the day for the date-number specified, @MONTH will display the number of the month, and @YEAR will display the number of the year.

 EXAMPLE: The cell A1 contains the formula @DATE(90,2,25) which produces a number that represents the date February 25, 1990. @DAY(+A1) will return the number 25. @MONTH(+A1) will return the number 2. @YEAR(+A1) will return the number 90.

BUILT-IN FUNCTIONS

Time Functions

@TIME(hour,minutes,seconds)
> display the time for the specified hour, minutes, and seconds.
>
> *EXAMPLE:* @TIME(16,20,10) will produce a number that represents the time 4:20:10 PM.

@HOUR(time-number)
@MINUTE(time-number)
@SECOND(time-number)
> @HOUR will display the hour of the time-number specified, @MINUTE will display the minute, and @SECOND will display the second.
>
> *EXAMPLE: The cell A1 contains the formula @TIME(16,20,10) which produces a number that represents the time 4:20:10 PM. @HOUR(+A1) will return the number 16. @MINUTE(+A1) will return the number 20. @SECOND(+A1) will return the number 10.*

Date or Time Function

@NOW
> produces the current date or time (depending on the cell format).

Conversion Functions

@DATEVALUE(string)
> produces a calculated date from a string that resembles a date.
>
> *EXAMPLE:* @DATEVALUE("25-Feb-90") produces the date number for the date February 25, 1990.

@TIMEVALUE(string)
> produces a calculated time from a string that resembles a time.
>
> *EXAMPLE:* @TIMEVALUE("04:20:10 PM") produces the time number for the time 4:20:10 PM.

This group of functions is used by typing the following into a cell:

@FUNCTION(argument

1. The first character typed must be the symbol **@**.
2. Type the **Function** name.

   EXAMPLE: **DATE**

3. Type the **arguments** (separated by commas if multiple arguments) within parentheses.

   NOTE: See each function for a list of arguments.

   EXAMPLE: The following formula would enter the date January 6, 1954:

   @DATE(54,1,6)

Financial Functions

@CTERM(interest,future-value,present-value)
   calculates the number of periods it will take for an amount to grow from a specified *present value* to a specified *future value* at a specified *interest* rate.

@DDB(cost,salvage,life,period)
   uses the double-declining balance method to calculate depreciation allowance (for a specified *period* over a specified *life*) of an asset purchased at a specified *cost* with a specified *salvage* value.

@FV(payments,interest,term)
   calculates the future value of an amount invested as specified *payments* over a specified term at a specified *interest* rate.

@IRR(guess,range)
   calculates the internal rate of return from an investment based on a series of cash flows which are stored in a specified *range* on the worksheet and a specified *guess* of what the internal rate of return might be.

BUILT-IN FUNCTIONS

@NPV(interest,range)
    calculates the net present value based on a series of cash flows which are stored in a specified *range* on the worksheet and a specified fixed *interest* rate.

@PMT(principle,interest,term)
    calculates the periodic payment for the specified *principal*, *interest*, and *term*.

@PV(payments,interest,term)
    calculates the present value of an amount invested as specified *payments* over a specified term at a specified *interest* rate.

@RATE(future-value,present-value,term)
    calculates the interest rate of an amount currently worth the specified present value, which will reach the specified *future value* in the specified *term*.

@SLN(cost,salvage,life)
    calculates straight-line depreciation (over a specified *life*) of an asset purchased at a specified *cost* with a specified *salvage* value. The number returned is the depreciation allowance for one period.

@SYD(cost,salvage,life,period)]
    calculates sum-of-the-years' digits depreciation (for a specified *period* over a specified *life*) of an asset purchased at a specified cost with a specified *salvage* value.

@TERM(payments,interest,future-value)
    calculates the term that it will take for an amount consisting of a specified number of *payments*, at a specified *interest* rate, to reach a specified *future value*.

    This group of functions is used by typing the following into a cell:

@FUNCTION(argument)

1. The first character typed must be the symbol **@** .
2. Type the **Function** name.

    EXAMPLE: **PMT**

3. Type the **arguments** (separated by commas if multiple arguments) within parentheses.

    NOTE: See each function for a list of arguments.

    EXAMPLE: To determine the monthly payment on a $10,000 five-year (60-month) loan at 12% interest.

    @PMT(10000,.12,60)

Mathematical Functions

@ABS(x)
returns the absolute value of a specified number (x).

@EXP(x)
value of *e* (approximately 2.718282) raised to the specified power (x).

@INT(x)
returns the integer value of a specified number (x). The integer value is *not* rounded (see @ROUND below).

@LN(x)
returns the natural logarithm of a specified number (x).

@LOG(x)
returns the common logarithm of a specified number (x).

@MOD(x,y)
returns the modulus (remainder) of the division of two specified numbers (x/y).

@RAND
returns a random number between 0 and 1.

BUILT-IN FUNCTIONS

@ROUND(x,n)
will round a specified number (x) to a specified number of decimal places (n). A negative number of decimal places will round to tens, hundreds, and so on.

EXAMPLE:

@ROUND(5452.54,-1) = 5450
@ROUND(5452.54,-2) = 5500

@SQRT(x)
returns the square root of a specified number (x).

Trigonometric Functions

@ACOS(x)
returns the arc cosine of a specified number (x).

@ASIN(x)
returns the arc sine of a specified number (x).

@ATAN(x)
returns the arc tangent of a specified number (x).

@ATAN2(x,y)
returns the four-quadrant arc tangent of two specified numbers (y/x).

@COS(x)
returns the cosine of a specified angle (x).

@PI
the value of PI (3.1415926536)

@SIN(x)
returns the sine of a specified angle (x).

@TAN(x)
returns the tangent of a specified angle (x).

This group of functions is used by typing the following into a cell:

@FUNCTION(argument)

1. The first character typed must be the symbol @ .
2. Type the **Function** name.

    EXAMPLE: **ROUND**

3. Type the **arguments** (separated by commas if multiple arguments) within parentheses.

    NOTE: See each function for a list of arguments.

    EXAMPLE: Cell A1 contains the value 3.589. @ROUND(+A1,0) returns 3.59

Statistical Functions

@AVG
  calculates average value in a specified list.

@COUNT
  counts non-blank cells in a specified list.

@MAX
  returns the maximum value in a specified list.

@MIN
  returns the minimum value in a specified list.

@STD
  returns the standard deviation in a specified list.

@SUM
  calculates the sum of values in a specified list.

@VAR
  finds the variance of values in a specified list.

All of these functions are used by typing the following into a cell:

@FUNCTION(list)

1. The first character typed must be the symbol @ .

2. Type the **Function** name.

   EXAMPLE: **AVG**

3. Type the **list** within parentheses. Items in the list must be separated by commas.

   The term *list* refers to a list of numbers, formulas, cell addresses, ranges, range names, or any combination of these elements.

   EXAMPLE:

   @AVG(A1..A10)
   @AVG(A1..A10,2345,A13)
   @AVG(range1,range2)

String Functions

String functions are used to manipulate character strings.

@CHAR(x)
returns the character that corresponds with the specified LICS code (x). For a list of codes, refer to the Lotus manual that was supplied with your system.

@CLEAN(string)
removes any control characters from the specified string.

@CODE(string)
returns the LICS code that corresponds with the first character in the specified string. For a list of codes, refer to the Lotus manual that was supplied with your system.

@EXACT(string1,string2)
compares two specified strings (string1 and string2). Returns a logical true (1) if the strings match. Returns a logical false (0) if the strings do not match.

@FIND(search,string,string,start-number)
locates a specified *search string* within a specified *string*. The command will begin searching the string with the specified character *start number*. When the search string is located, the system will return the character number of the first character of that string.

EXAMPLE: @FIND("Pete","Mr Peter Dean",0) will return 4 due to the fact that the first character in the search string (P) appears as the fourth character in the string.

EXAMPLE: @FIND("a","abcdefgabc",5) will return 8. Since the specified start number is 5, the system begins to search the string at character 5. Therefore, it skips over the "a" that is found at position 1 in the string.

@LEFT(string,n)
returns a specified number of characters (n) that appear in a specified string. The system counts characters from the first character in the string.

EXAMPLE: @LEFT("abcdef",3) returns the string "abc".

@LENGTH(string)
returns the length (number of characters) in a specified string.

@LOWER(string)
returns lower-case of the specified string.

EXAMPLE: If the cell A1 contains the string ABCDE, then @LOWER(+A1) = abcde.

@MID(string,start-number,n)
returns a specified number of characters (n) that appear in a specified string beginning with the character position of the start number.

EXAMPLE: @LEFT("abcdef",3,2) returns the string "cd".

@N(range)
    returns a zero (0) if the first cell in the specified range is a label; or if the first cell in the specified range is a value, returns the value in that cell.

@PROPER(string)
    returns proper case (initial capitalization) of the specified string.

    EXAMPLE: If the cell A1 contains the string MR. JOHN DOE, @PROPER(+A1) = Mr. John Doe.

@REPEAT(string,n)
    repeats the string a specified number of times (n).

@REPLACE(original-string,start-number,n,new-string)
    replaces characters in the *original string* with characters specified as a *new string*. Replaces a specified number of characters (n) beginning with the specified character *start number*.

    EXAMPLE: @REPLACE("Mrs. Smith",0,3,"Dr") returns the string "Dr. Smith".

@RIGHT(string,n)
    returns a specified number of characters (n) that appear in a specified string. The system counts characters from the last character in the string.

    EXAMPLE: @RIGHT("abcdef",3) returns the string "def".

@S(range)
    If the first cell in the specified range is a label, returns that label; or if the first cell in the specified range is a value, returns a null (empty) string.

@STRING(x,n)
    converts a specified value (x) into a string with a specified number of decimal places (n).

    EXAMPLE: @STRING(1/3,2) = ".33".

@TRIM(string)

trims leading or trailing blanks from a specified string.

@UPPER(string)

returns uppercase of the specified string.

EXAMPLE: If the cell A1 contains the string abcde, @LOWER(+A1) = ABCDE.

@VALUE(string)

converts a specified string into a value that can be used for calculation.

EXAMPLE: @VALUE("123") produces the value 123.

This group of functions is used by typing the following into a cell:

@FUNCTION(argument)

1. The first character typed must be the symbol @ .
2. Type the **Function** name.

   EXAMPLE: **LEFT**

3. Type the **arguments** (separated by commas if multiple arguments) within parentheses.

   NOTE: See each function for a list of arguments.

   NOTE: When specifying a string, you may specify a cell address or range name of a cell that contains a string. You may also type the string itself, however, the string must appear delimited within quotes.

   EXAMPLE: If A1 contains the string "abcdef" and the range name RANGE1:

   @LEFT(A1,3) = abc
   @LEFT(range1,3) = abc
   @LEFT("range1",3) = ran

Logical Functions

@FALSE
returns the logical false (0).

@IF(condition,x,y)
If a specified *condition* (a formula that you will input) is TRUE, the function returns whatever is specified as *x*. If the condition is FALSE, the function returns whatever is specified as *y*.

@ISAAF(name)
tests for a specified add-in @function. If the *named* function is present, @ISAAF returns a logical true (1). If the function is not present, @ISAAF returns a logical false (0).

@ISAAP(name)
tests for a specified attached add-in. If the *named* add-in is present, @ISAAP returns a logical true (1). If the add-in is not present, @ISAAP returns a logical false (0).

@ISERR(x)
tests a specified string, value, cell location, or condition (x) for an error (ERR). If the tested item is ERR, a @ISERR returns a logical true (1). If not, @ISERR returns a logical false (0).

NOTE: See page 42 for more information about @ERR.

@ISNA(x)
tests a specified string, value, cell location, or condition (x) for NA (not available). If the tested item is NA, a @ISNA returns a logical true (1). If not, @ISNA returns a logical false (0).

NOTE: See page 43 for more information about @NA.

@ISNUMBER(x)
tests whether or not a specified string, value, cell location, or condition (x) is a number. If the tested item is a number, a @ISNUMBER returns a logical

true (1). If not, @ISNUMBER returns a logical false (0).

@ISSTRING(x)

tests whether or not a specified string, value, cell location, or condition (x) is a string. If the tested item is a number, a @ISSTRING returns a logical true (1). If not, @ISSTRING returns a logical false (0).

@TRUE

returns the logical true (1).

This group of functions is used by typing the following into a cell:

@FUNCTION(argument)

1. The first character typed must be the symbol @ .
2. Type the **Function** name.

    EXAMPLE: **IF**

3. Type the **arguments** (separated by commas if multiple arguments) within parentheses.

    NOTE: See each function for a list of arguments.

    EXAMPLE: The following formula will test cell A1. If the value in A1 is greater than or equal to 10000, the @IF function will return the result of the formula A1*.05. If the value in cell A1 is less than 10000, the @IF function will return the result of the formula A1*.1)

    @IF(A1=1000,A1*.05,A1*.1)

Special Functions

@@(location)

returns the contents of a specified *location*. The location can be a cell address or range name of a single cell.

@CELL(attribute,range)

returns specific information about the first cell in a specified *range*. The information returned is determined by the *attribute* that is specified.

The following attributes can be specified:

Attribute	Returns	
address	cell address	
col	column letter	
contents	cell contents	
filename	current spreadsheet path and filename	
format	cell format:	
	C0 thru C15	currency format—the number represents the number of decimal places
	F0 thru F15	fixed
	G	general
	P0 thru P15	percent
	S0 thru S15	scientific
	,0 thru ,15	comma
	+	+/-
	D1 thru D9	date (see page 51)
	T	text
	H	Hidden
prefix	cell label prefix	
protect	whether protect is on (1) or off (0)	
row	row number	
type	data type in cell (b = blank, v = value, l = label)	
width	column width	

@CELLPOINTER(attribute)

returns specific information about the cell in which the pointer is located. The information returned is determined by the *attribute* that is specified. See above for a list of attributes.

@CHOOSE(offset,list)

returns an item within a specified *list*. The item returned will be determined by the *offset* number of that item in the list. The first item in the list has an offset number of 0, the second has an offset number of 1, and so on.

NOTE: The *list* can consist of numbers, formulas, cell addresses, ranges, range names, or any combination of these elements. Items in the list must be separated by commas.

@COLS(range)

returns the number of columns in a specified **range.**

@ERR

returns the Lotus error message (ERR).

NOTE: The error message is also returned by the system whenever formulas or conditions exist that cause an error, such as dividing a value by zero.

@HLOOKUP(x,range,row)

returns an item that appears in a table by performing a horizontal lookup. The function will search through the first row of a table that appears within the specified *range*. When it finds the value specified as *x*, it will then count down the specified number of *rows* and will return the contents of that cell.

EXAMPLE: The following table appears within the range A1..D4:

New York	Los Angeles	Chicago	Seattle
1,405	12,345	3,495	334
3,485	2,245	2,495	1,345
34,294	9,345	5,697	465

The formula @HLOOKUP("Chicago",A1..D4,2) will return the value 2,495.

@INDEX(range,column-offset,row-offset)

returns an item that appears in a table. The function will search through the table that appears within the specified *range*. It will count across the specified *column offset*. It will then count down the specified *row offset* and will return the contents of that cell.

NOTE: The first item in the row or column has an offset number of 0, the second has an offset number of 1, and so on.

@NA

returns the Lotus "not available" message (ERR).

@ROWS(range)

returns the number of rows in a specified ***range.***

@VLOOKUP(x,range,column)

returns an item that appears in a table by performing a vertical lookup. The function will search through the first column of a table that appears within the specified *range*. When it finds the value specified as *x*, it will then count across the specified number of *columns* and will return the contents of that cell.

EXAMPLE: The following table appears within the range A1..D4:

New York	1,405	12,345	3,495
Los Angeles	3,485	2,245	2,495
Chicago	34,294	9,345	5,697
Seattle	334	1,345	465

The formula @VLOOKUP("Chicago",A1..D4,2) will return the value 9,345.

This group of functions is used by typing the following into a cell:

@FUNCTION(argument)

1. The first character typed must be the symbol **@** .
2. Type the **Function** name.

    EXAMPLE: **CELL**

3. Type the **arguments** (separated by commas if multiple arguments) within parentheses.

    NOTE: See each function for a list of arguments.

FORMATTING

Format Commands

Format commands affect the way cell entries appear on the worksheet. There are two types of format commands: *range* and *global*.

- **RANGE FORMAT** Changes appearance of a specified *range* of cells.
- **GLOBAL FORMAT** Changes appearance of ALL cells on worksheet. A *global* format command will not affect cells that have been given a local (range) format.

NOTE: Most format commands can be used to format either a range of cells or all the entries on the sheet.

Global Format — /WGF

Any *global* format command affects ALL entries on the worksheet, except those cells that have been given a local (range) format.

To give a global format command:

1. Press the SLASH (**/**) key.

   The Main Menu will appear.

2. Type **W** to select **W**orksheet.

   The Worksheet Menu will appear.

3. Type **G** to select **G**lobal.

   The Global Menu and Global Settings Screen will appear.

4. Type **F** to select **F**ormat.

   The Format Menu will appear.

5. Select the desired format menu item (see page 47).

6. If the prompt "Enter number of decimal places (0..15)" appears

   a. Type the desired number of decimal places.

   b. Press **ENTER**.

The global format selected will be enabled.

Range Format — /RF

Range format commands affect one cell or a specified range of cells. To give a RANGE FORMAT command:

1. Position the pointer over the first cell to format.

2. Press the SLASH (/) key.

   The Main Menu will appear.

3. Type **R** to select **R**ange.

   The Range Menu will appear.

4. Type **F** to select **F**ormat.

   The Format Menu will appear.

5. Select the desired format menu item (see page 47).

6. If the prompt "Enter number of decimal places (0..15)" appears

   a. Type the desired number of decimal places.

   b. Press **ENTER**.

   The prompt "Enter range to format" will appear.

7. Point to (or type) the range of cells to be formatted (see page 4).

8. Press **ENTER** to accept the range.

    The range format selected will be enabled. Cells that have been given a Range Format will not be affected by Global Format commands.

Format Menu Selections

Menu Item	Formats cell entries to:
FIXED	Fixed number of decimal places (page 48).
SCIENTIFIC	Exponential format (page 48).
CURRENCY	Dollar sign, commas, specified number of decimal places (page 49).
,	Commas, negative values in parentheses (page 49).
GENERAL	As input (page 50).
+/-	Horizontal bar graph (page 50).
PERCENT	Percent sign, specified number of decimal places (page 50).
DATE	Date format (page 51).
TEXT	Displays formulas instead of values (page 52).
HIDDEN	Hides a range of cells. A hidden range will not display or print (page 52).
RESET	Resets range to global cell format (page 52).

NOTE: If a value or the result of a formula contains more digits than will fit in a column, a line of asterisks will appear. To change the width of the column, see pages 56–58.

Fixed Format

- Affects values and the results of formulas.

- Allows you to set a fixed number of decimal places.

- Negative values will appear preceded by a minus sign.

- The letter F and the number of decimal places set will appear next to the cell address whenever the pointer rests on a cell that has been given a fixed range format.

- For information on setting a global fixed format, see page 45. For information on setting a range fixed format, see page 46.

Scientific Format

- Affects values and the results of formulas.

- Displays numbers in exponential scientific notation.

- Allows you to set a fixed number of decimal places.

- Negative values will appear with the exponent preceded by a minus sign.

- The letter S and the number of decimal places set will appear next to the cell address whenever the pointer rests on a cell that has been given a scientific range format.

- For information on setting a global scientific format, see page 45. For information on setting a range scientific format, see page 46.

Currency Format

- Affects values and the results of formulas.
- Inserts a dollar sign before the entry.
- Negative values appear within parentheses.
- Allows you to set a fixed number of decimal places.
- The letter C and the number of decimal places set will appear next to the cell address whenever the pointer rests on a cell that has been given a currency range format.
- For information on setting a global currency format, see page 45. For information on setting a range currency format, see page 46.

Comma (,) Format

- Affects values and the results of formulas.
- Inserts commas.
- Negative values appear in parentheses.
- Allows you to set fixed number of decimal places.
- A comma and the number of decimal places set will appear next to the cell address whenever the pointer rests on a cell that has been given a comma range format.
- For information on setting a global comma format, see page 45. For information on setting a range comma format, see page 46.

General Format

The General Format is the default format. It displays entries as they were input:

- Values appear without commas, carried out to as many decimal places as necessary.
- The result of formulas appear without commas, carried out to as many decimal places as necessary.
- The label-prefix is set at left-justify.
- For information on setting a global general format, see page 45. For information on setting a range general format, see page 46.

Horizontal Bar Graph (+/-) Format

- Affects values and the results of formulas.
- Creates a horizontal bar graph of plus signs for positive numbers.
- Creates a horizontal bar graph of minus signs for negative numbers.
- A plus sign will appear next to the cell address whenever the pointer rests on a cell that has been given a +/- range format.
- For information on setting a global +/- format, see page 45. For information on setting a range +/- format, see page 46.

Percent Format

- Affects values and the results of formulas.
- Displays numbers as percentages.

- Allows you to set a fixed number of decimal places.

- Negative values will appear preceded by a minus sign.

- The letter P and the number of decimal places set will appear next to the cell address whenever the pointer rests on a cell that has been given a percent range format.

- For information on setting a global percent format, see page 45. For information on setting a range percent format, see page 46.

Date Format

The Date Format causes numbers to be displayed as dates or time. These numbers can be input with the @NOW or @DATE built-in functions (see pages 28–29).

The following date formats are available:

1	(DD-MM-YY)
2	(DD-MMM)
3	(MMM-YY)
4	(Long Intn'l)
5	(Short Intn'l)

Time

The following time formats are available:

1	(HH:MM:SS AM/PM)
2	(HH:MM AM/PM)
3	(Long Intn'l)
4	(Short Intn'l)

The format that appears for the Long Intn'l and Short Intn'l Date and Time selections can be set with the **/W**orksheet **G**lobal **D**efaults **O**ther **I**nternational command (see page 113).

Text Format

- Displays *formulas* instead of formula *results*.
- All formulas that do not fit in cells are truncated.
- Values will return to general (as input) format.
- The letter T will appear next to the cell address whenever the pointer rests on a cell that has been given a text range format.
- For information on setting a global text format, see page 45. For information on setting a range text format, see page 46.

Hidden Format

- The contents of hidden cells will not display on the screen or print.
- For information on setting a global hidden format, see page 45. For information on setting a range hidden format, see page 46.

Reset Format

- Returns a range of cells to any global format that has been set.
- For information on resetting a range format, see page 46.

Range Label-Prefix — /RL

The RANGE LABEL-PREFIX command allows you to change the label prefix of a range of cells. Once the command is given, all label cells in the range will appear left-justified, right-justified, or centered.

FORMATTING

1. Position the pointer over the first cell to format.
2. Press the SLASH (/) key.

    The Main Menu will appear.

3. Type **R** to select **R**ange.

    The Range Menu will appear.

4. Type **L** to select **L**abel-Prefix.

    The Label-Prefix Menu will appear.

5. Type one of the following:
    - **L** to select **L**eft-Justified (labels will align with the left side of the cell).
    - **R** to select **R**ight-Justified (labels will align with the right side of the cell).
    - **C** to select **C**entered (labels will appear centered within the cell).

    The prompt "Enter range of labels" will appear.

6. Point to (or type) the range of cells to be formatted (see page 4).
7. Press **ENTER** to accept the range.

    The label prefix selected will be enabled.

Global Label-Prefix — /WGL

The LABEL-PREFIX command allows you to change the default label prefix to left, right, or center. All labels will be left-justified, right-justified, or centered when typed on worksheet. The command does not affect labels that have already been input.

1. Press the SLASH (/) key.

    The Main Menu will appear.

2. Type **W** to select **W**orksheet.

    The Worksheet Menu will appear.

3. Type **G** to select **Global**.

   The Global Menu and Global Settings Screen will appear.

4. Type **L** to select **L**abel-Prefix.

   The Label-Prefix Menu will appear.

5. Type one of the following:
   - **L** to select **L**eft-Justified (labels will align with the left side of the cell).
   - **R** to select **R**ight-Justified (labels will align with the right side of the cell).
   - **C** to select **C**entered (labels will appear centered within the cell).

   The label prefix selected will become the default for newly typed label. All labels that already appear on the worksheet will not be affected. To change the label prefix of labels already on the worksheet, use the Range Label-Prefix command (page 52).

Zero Suppression — /WGZ

The system can be set so that a zero (0), a blank, or any specified label can appear in any cell instead of the value zero. To set zero suppression:

1. Press the SLASH (**/**) key.

   The Main Menu will appear.

2. Type **W** to select **W**orksheet.

   The Worksheet Menu will appear.

3. Type **G** to select **G**lobal.

   The Global Menu and Global Settings Screen will appear.

FORMATTING

4. Type **Z** to select **Z**ero.

   The Zero Suppression Menu will appear.

5. Select one of the following:

   - Type **N** (**N**o) to tell the system *not* to suppress zeros (any zero will appear within a cell),
   - Type **Y** (**Y**es) to tell the system to suppress zeros (cells containing the value zero will appear blank), or
   - Type **L** to select a **L**abel to appear instead of the value zero. If Label is selected, the prompt "Enter label (can include label prefix):" will appear. Type the desired label and press **ENTER**.

   The system will return to the READY mode.

Range Justify — /RJ

The command format a cell containing a long label entry so that the entry appears blocked into a range of cells that you specify. To use the RANGE JUSTIFY command:

1. Position the pointer over the first cell to format.
2. Press the SLASH (/) key.

   The Main Menu will appear.

3. Type **R** to select **R**ange.

   The Range Menu will appear.

4. Type **J** to select **J**ustify.

   The prompt "Enter justify range" will appear.

5. Point to (or type) the range of cells in which justified text will appear (see page 4).
6. Press **ENTER** to accept the range.

NOTE: If the text will not fit into the range specified, the message "Justify range is full or line too long" will appear. Press **ESC** to clear the message.

Column Width (Individual Columns) — /WC

Default column width is nine characters. Labels that are longer than the column width will fill adjacent unoccupied columns, and will be truncated if the adjacent column is occupied. Values and formula results that are longer than column width will appear in either exponential notation or as a row of asterisks.

To reset the width of one column:

1. Press the SLASH (**/**) key.

   The Main Menu will appear.

2. Type **W** to select **W**orksheet.

   The Worksheet Menu will appear.

3. Type **C** to select **C**olumn.

   The Column Menu will appear.

4. Type one of the following:
   - **S** to select **S**et-Width. This will allow you to select a column width.
   - **R** to select **R**eset-Width. This will reset the default column width. Disregard Steps 5 and 6 below.

   The prompt "Enter column width (1-240)" will appear.

5. Type the new column width setting, or use the **Left** or **Right Arrow** key to adjust the width.

6. Press **ENTER** to accept the column width setting.

FORMATTING

NOTE: To adjust column width of a range of columns, see below. To hide or display a column, see page 59. To adjust global column width, see page 58.

Column Width (Range of Columns) — /WCC

The default column width is nine characters. Labels that are longer than the column width will fill adjacent unoccupied columns, and will be truncated if the adjacent column is occupied. Values and formula results that are longer than column width will appear in either exponential notation or as a row of asterisks.

To reset the width of a range of columns:

1. Press the SLASH (/) key.

   The Main Menu will appear.

2. Type **W** to select **W**orksheet.

   The Worksheet Menu will appear.

3. Type **C** to select **C**olumn.

   The Column Menu will appear.

4. Type **C** to select **C**olumn-Range.

   The Column-Range Menu will appear.

5. Type one of the following:
   - **S** to select **S**et-Width. This will allow you to select a width for the range of columns.
   - **R** to select **R**eset-Width. This will reset the default column width. Disregard Steps 6 through 9 below.

   The prompt "Enter range for column width change" will appear.

6. Point to (or type) the range of columns to be affected (see page 4).

7. Press **ENTER** to accept the range.

   The prompt "Select a width for range of columns (1-240)" will appear.

8. Type the new column width setting, or use the **Left** or **Right Arrow** key to adjust the width.

9. Press **ENTER** to accept the column width setting.

   NOTE: To adjust column width of an individual column, see page 56. To hide or display a column, see page 59. To adjust global column width, see below.

Global Column Width — /WGC

The GLOBAL COLUMN WIDTH command is used to change the width of ALL column on the worksheet. It will not, however, change the width of any columns that have individual column widths (/WC command page 56 or /WCC command page 57).

1. Press the SLASH (/) key.

   The Main Menu will appear.

2. Type **W** to select **W**orksheet.

   The Worksheet Menu will appear.

3. Type **G** to select **G**lobal.

   The Global Menu and Global Settings Screen will appear.

4. Type **C** to select **C**olumn

   The prompt "Enter global column width (1-240)" will appear.

5. Type the new column width setting, or use the **Left** or **Right Arrow** key to adjust the width.

FORMATTING

6. Press **ENTER** to accept the column width setting.

   NOTE: To adjust column width of a single column, see page 56. To adjust column width of a range of columns, see page 57. To hide or display a column, see below.

Hide/Display Columns — /WCH, /WCD

The contents of a hidden column will not display on the screen or print. To hide or display a column:

1. Press the SLASH (/) key.

   The Main Menu will appear.

2. Type **W** to select **W**orksheet.

   The Worksheet Menu will appear.

3. Type **C** to select **C**olumn

   The Column Menu will appear.

4. Type one of the following:

   - **H** to select **H**ide.
   - **D** to select **D**isplay.

   The prompt "Specify column hide" or "Specify the column to display" will appear.

6. Point to (or type) the range of columns to be hidden or displayed (see page 4).

7. Press **ENTER** to accept the range.

   NOTE: To adjust column width of an individual column, see page 56. To adjust column width of a range of columns, see page 57. To adjust global column width, see page 58.

Titles Command — /WT

The TITLES command locks titles in place so that they are always on the screen. Either HORIZONTAL, VERTICAL, or BOTH horizontal and vertical titles can be locked in place. Titles can be unlocked with the CLEAR TITLES command.

To lock or clear titles:

1. Position the pointer:

   Before the command to lock is given, the pointer should be positioned to the right of the column to lock (if you are locking VERTICAL titles) or below the last row of titles to lock (if you are locking HORIZONTAL titles).

2. Press the SLASH (**/**) key.

   The Main Menu will appear.

3. Type **W** to select **W**orksheet.

   The Worksheet Menu will appear.

4. Type **T** to select **T**itles.

   The Titles Menu will appear.

5. Type one of the following:

   - **B** to select **B**oth (lock both horizontal and vertical titles).
   - **H** to select **H**orizontal (lock horizontal titles).
   - **V** to select **V**ertical (lock vertical titles).
   - **C** to select **C**lear (clear previously locked titles).

   When titles are locked, the **HOME** key will move the pointer to upper left cell that is below and to the right of locked titles. The **Arrow** keys will not move the pointer into the locked title area. Only the **F5** key (GO TO) will move pointer to cells within locked title. (See page 18 for more information about the **F5** key.)

Window Command — /WW

The WINDOW command will split the display either horizontally or vertically into two separate windows, allowing you to view two different sections of worksheet simultaneously. This is very valuable if you want to change a figure in one part of the worksheet and immediately see the effects of that change in another part of the sheet. The display can be returned to a single window with the WINDOW CLEAR command.

1. Position the pointer:

   Before the command to split is given, the pointer should be positioned in the column or row where you want the split to appear.

2. Press the SLASH (**/**) key.

   The Main Menu will appear.

3. Type **W** to select **W**orksheet.

   The Worksheet Menu will appear.

4. Type **W** to select **W**indows.

   The Windows Menu will appear.

5. Type one of the following:

   - **H** to select **H**orizontal (split the window horizontally).
   - **V** to select **V**ertical (split the window vertically).
   - **S** to select **S**ynchronize (synchronize window movement).
   - **U** to select **U**nsynchronize (unsynchronize window movement).
   - **C** to select **C**lear (clear previously split window).

   NOTE: When window is split, scrolling in the direction of the split is synchronized. Scrolling can be unsynchronized and synchronized by giving the WINDOW UNSYNCHRONIZE and WINDOW SYNCHRONIZE commands (see above).

The **F6** key will move pointer from one window to another. The **HOME**, **F5** (GO TO), and directional **ARROW** keys will only move the pointer within the current window.

Global Worksheet Protection — /WGP

Worksheet protection allows you to protect all cells in a worksheet against accidental changes. Nothing can be typed into cells which are protected.

Global worksheet protection can be turned OFF by using the Global Protection Disable command.

1. Press the SLASH (/) key.

    The Main Menu will appear.

2. Type **W** to select **W**orksheet.

    The Worksheet Menu will appear.

3. Type **G** to select **G**lobal.

    The Global Menu and Global Settings Screen will appear.

4. Type **P** to select **P**rotect.

    The Protect Menu will appear.

5. Type one of the following:
    - **E** to select **E**nable (turn worksheet protection ON).
    - **D** to select **D**isable (turn worksheet protection OFF).

    When Global Protection is enabled, the letters PR will appear next to the cell address whenever the pointer rests on a cell that is not range unprotected (see page 63).

    NOTE: To allow input in one cell or a range of cells, use the "Range Unprotect" command (see page 63).

Range Unprotect/Protect — /RU, /RP

While Global Worksheet Protection is enabled, one cell or range of cells can be unprotected to allow input. An unprotected cell or range of cells can be protected again by using the RANGE PROTECT command.

1. Position the pointer over the first cell in the range to protect or unprotect.
2. Press the SLASH (**/**) key.

   The Main Menu will appear.
3. Type **R** to select **R**ange.

   The Range Menu will appear.
4. Type one of the following:
   - **U** to select **U**nprotect (unprotect the range)
   - **P** to select **P**rotect (protect the range)

   The prompt "Enter range to unprotect" or "Enter range to protect" will appear.
5. Point to (or type) the range to be protected or unprotected (see page 4).
6. Press **ENTER** to accept the range.

   Unprotected cells appear either in a different color or brighter on screen. The letter U appears next to the cell address whenever the pointer is positioned over an unprotected cell.

   NOTE: The RANGE INPUT command will move the pointer only to unprotected cells when one of the **Arrow** keys is pressed. For more information on Range Input, see page 46.

EDITING

General Information

Any spreadsheet that is stored on a disk can be edited. To edit a file, a copy of the file must first be retrieved from the disk (see page 78).

After editing a file, the changes exist only on the screen and in the system's memory. If you want to save the edited version, you must use the FILE SAVE command (see page 76).

Erase Worksheet — /WE

When the worksheet is erased it is cleared from the screen and internal memory. However, this command does not change the copy of the worksheet that is stored on the disk.

To erase a worksheet:

1. Press the SLASH (/) key.

   The Main Menu will appear.

2. Type **W** to select **W**orksheet.

   The Worksheet Menu will appear.

3. Type **E** to select **E**rase.

   A menu will appear with the selections No and Yes.

4. Either:
   - Type **Y** to select **Y**es and erase the worksheet from the screen, or
   - Type **N** to select **N**o and cancel the worksheet erase command.

   The blank worksheet grid will appear.

NOTE: To erase a *Range* of cells within a worksheet, see page 66.

Delete Column/Row — /WD

The DELETE command deletes an entire column or row from the screen and memory. After the deletion, all columns or rows move to fill in the gap left by the deleted column/row and all formulas adjust to reflect their new positions on the sheet.

Once a column/row is deleted, it CANNOT be recalled to the screen unless UNDO is active (see page 72 for information on UNDO).

To delete a column or row:

1. Position the pointer anywhere within the first column or row to delete.
2. Press the SLASH (/) key.

    The Main Menu will appear.

3. Type **W** to select **W**orksheet.

    The Worksheet Menu will appear.

4. Type **D** to select **D**elete.

    The Delete Menu will appear.

5. Either:
    - Type **C** to delete a **C**olumn, or
    - Type **R** to delete a **R**ow.

    The prompt "Enter range of columns (rows) to delete" will appear.

6. Point to (or type) the range or columns or rows to be deleted (see page 4).

NOTE: You need only specify one cell in each column or row. For example, specifying the range A1..A3 will delete rows 1 through 3. Specifying the range A1..C1 will delete columns A through C.

7. Press **ENTER** to accept the range.

NOTE: You must make sure you do not delete cells that are referenced by formulas that will remain on the worksheet after the deletion. If you do, an ERROR message will appear in the cells containing those referenced formulas after deletion.

Range Erase — /RE

The ERASE command will erase one cell, a part of a row or column, or a range of cells that covers several rows and/or columns.

Nothing on the worksheet moves after the erase. Empty space is left "as is." Since no rows or columns move, no formulas are adjusted.

Once a cell or a range of cells is erased it CANNOT be recalled to the screen unless UNDO is active (see page 72 for information on UNDO).

To erase a range:

1. Position the pointer over the first cell to erase.
2. Press the SLASH (/) key.

   The Main Menu will appear.
3. Type **R** to select **R**ange.

   The Range Menu will appear.
4. Type **E** to select **E**rase.

   The prompt "Enter range to erase" will appear.

5. Point to (or type) the range of cells to be erased (see page 4).

6. Press **ENTER** to accept the range.

   NOTE: To erase an entire worksheet, see page 64.

Insert Column/Row — /WI

The INSERT command inserts one or more blank columns or rows on the worksheet. After the insertion, all columns or rows move to make space for the inserted columns or rows; and all formulas adjust to reflect their new positions on the sheet.

1. Position the pointer in the location where the first column or row is to appear.

2. Press the SLASH (**/**) key.

   The Main Menu will appear.

3. Type **W** to select **W**orksheet.

   The Worksheet Menu will appear.

4. Type **I** to select **I**nsert.

   The Insert Menu will appear.

5. Either:
   - Type **C** to insert a **C**olumn, or
   - Type **R** to insert a **R**ow.

   The prompt "Enter column (row) insert range" will appear.

6. Point to (or type) the range or columns or rows to be inserted (see page 4).

   NOTE: You need only specify one cell in each column or row. For example, specifying the range A1..A3 will insert blank rows 1 through 3. Specifying the range A1..C1 will insert blank columns A through C.

7. Press **ENTER** to accept the range.

Copy — /C

The COPY command copies one cell or a range of cells to any location on worksheet.

Copied formulas will adjust relative to their new positions on the worksheet, unless the formula contains absolute values (see page 26).

1. Position the pointer over the first cell to copy FROM.
2. Press the SLASH (/) key.

   The Main Menu will appear.
3. Type **C** to select **C**opy.

   The prompt "Enter range to copy FROM" will appear.
4. Point to (or type) the range of cells to be copied (see pages 4, 71).
5. Press **ENTER**.

   The prompt "Enter range to copy TO" will appear.
6. Point to (or type) the range to copy to (see page 71).
7. Press **ENTER**.

   NOTE: For information on moving a cell or range of cells, see page 70.

Range Value — /RV

The RANGE VALUE command will copy a range of cells that contain formulas and convert these formulas to values in the new location. To use range value:

1. Position the pointer over the first cell to copy FROM.
2. Press the SLASH (/) key.

   The Main Menu will appear.

EDITING

3. Type **R** to select **R**ange.

   The Range Menu will appear.

4. Type **V** to select **V**alue.

   The prompt "Enter range to copy FROM" will appear.

5. Point to (or type) the range of cells to be copied (see pages 4, 71).

6. Press **ENTER**.

   The prompt "Enter range to copy TO" will appear.

7. Point to (or type) the range to copy to (see page 71).

8. Press **ENTER**.

Range Transpose — /RT

The RANGE TRANSPOSE command will copy a range of cells, but will transpose the columns and rows in the new location. To use this command:

1. Position the pointer over the first cell to copy FROM.

2. Press the SLASH (**/**) key.

   The Main Menu will appear.

3. Type **R** to select **R**ange.

   The Range Menu will appear.

4. Type **T** to select **T**ranspose.

   The prompt "Enter range to copy FROM" will appear.

5. Point to (or type) the range of cells to be copied (see pages 4, 71).

6. Press **ENTER** to accept the range.

   The prompt "Enter range to copy TO" will appear.

7. Point to (or type) the range to copy to (see pages 4, 71).

8. Press **ENTER** to accept the range.

Move — /M

The MOVE command will move a cell or range of cells to any location on the worksheet.

Moved formulas will adjust relative to their new positions on the worksheet, unless the formula contains absolute values (see page 26).

After you move cells, the area that you have moved the cells FROM will appear blank.

1. Position the pointer over the first cell to move.

2. Press the SLASH (/) key.

   The Main Menu will appear.

3. Type **M** to select **M**ove.

   The prompt "Enter range to move FROM" will appear.

4. Point to (or type) the range of cells to be moved (see pages 4, 71).

5. Press **ENTER**.

   The prompt "Enter range to move TO" will appear.

6. Point to (or type) the range to move to (see pages 4, 71).

7. Press **ENTER**.

   NOTE: If you move TO cells that already contain entries, these entries will be replaced by the information that you have moved.

To MOVE information to a column or row without deleting the existing information in that column or row:

EDITING

1. INSERT a BLANK column or row at the move TO location (see page 67).
2. MOVE the information to the blank column or row.
3. DELETE the column or row that is left blank after the move (see page 65).

   NOTE: For information on copying a cell or range of cells, see pages 4, and below.

Specifying "Copy To" and "Move To" Range

When specifying the range to copy or move TO, results are obtained as follows:

FROM	TO	RESULT
A1..A3	**B1**	**B1..B3**
A1	B1	B1
A2		B2
A3		B3

FROM	TO	RESULT
A1..A3	**B1..D1**	**B1..D3**
A1	B1 C1 D1	B1 C1 D1
A2		B2 C2 D2
A3		B3 C3 D3

FROM	TO	RESULT
A1..C1	**A2**	**A2..C4**
A1 B1 C1	A2	A2 B2 C2

FROM	TO	RESULT
A1..C1	**A2..A4**	**A2..C4**
A1 B1 C1	A2	A2 B2 C2
	A3	A3 B3 C3
	A4	A4 B4 C4

Undo — ALT+F4

The UNDO key will allow you to undo any change that has been made since the last time the system was in the READY mode. The UNDO key will only operate if Undo has been Enabled (see below). To use Undo:

1. Hold **ALT** and press **F4**.

    The worksheet will return to its status at the last "Ready." To Undo the Undo,

2. Hold **ALT** and press **F4** again.

Disable/Enable Undo — /WGDOU

Changes made to the worksheet can be reversed by using the **ALT+F4** (UNDO) key only when the Undo feature is enabled. To enable Undo:

1. Press the SLASH (/) key.

    The Main Menu will appear.

2. Type **W** to select **W**orksheet.

    The Worksheet Menu will appear.

3. Type **G** to select **G**lobal.

    The Global Menu and Global Settings Screen will appear.

4. Type **D** to select **D**efault.

    The Default Menu and screen will appear.

5. Type **O** to select **O**ther.

    The Other Menu will appear.

6. Type **U** to select **U**ndo.

    The Undo Menu will appear.

EDITING

7. Type one of the following:
   - **E** to select **E**nable Undo (turn the Undo feature ON).
   - **D** to select **D**isable (turn the Undo feature OFF).

The system will return to the "Ready" mode.

Range Search — /RS(F,L,B)F

The range search command will search through a specified range for a specified character string. To use this command:

1. Press the SLASH (/) key.

   The Main Menu will appear.

2. Type **R** to select **R**ange.

   The Range Menu will appear.

3. Type **S** to select **S**earch.

   The prompt "Enter range to search" will appear.

4. Point to (or type) the range of cells through which to search.

5. Press **ENTER** to accept the range.

   The prompt "Enter string to search for" will appear.

6. Type the string to search for and press ENTER.

   NOTE: The string *does not* have to be delimited.

   The Search Menu will appear.

7. Select one of the following:
   - Type **F** to search only the **F**ormulas that appear within the range, or
   - Type **L** to search only the **L**abels that appear within the range, or

- Type **B** to search **B**oth formulas and labels.

The Find or Replace Menu will appear.

8. Type **F** to select **F**ind.

The system will search for and highlight the first instance of the string. A menu will appear with the selections "Next" and "Quit."

9. Select one of the following:
    - Type **N** to find the **N**ext instance of the string, or
    - Type **Q** to **Q**uit the procedure.

NOTE: The message "String not found" will appear after the last instance of the string is found, or if no instance of the string is found.

Range Search and Replace — /RS(F,L,B)R

The RANGE SEARCH AND REPLACE command will search through a specified range for a specified character string. It will then give you the option to replace that string with another string. To use this command:

1. Press the SLASH (/) key.

   The Main Menu will appear.

2. Type **R** to select **R**ange.

   The Range Menu will appear.

3. Type **S** to select **S**earch.

   The prompt "Enter range to search" will appear.

4. Point to (or type) the range of cells through which to search.

5. Press **ENTER** to accept the range.

   The prompt "Enter string to search for" will appear.

EDITING

6. Type the string to search for and press **ENTER**.

   NOTE: The string *does not* have to be delimited.

   The Search Menu will appear.

7. Select one of the following:
   - Type **F** to search only the **F**ormulas that appear within the range, or
   - Type **L** to search only the **L**abels that appear within the range, or
   - Type **B** to search **B**oth formulas and labels.

   The Find or Replace Menu will appear.

8. Type **R** to select **R**eplace.

   The prompt "Enter replacement string" will appear.

9. Type the string to search for and press **ENTER**.

   NOTE: The string *does not* have to be delimited.

The system will search for and highlight the first instance of the string. A menu will appear with the selections "Replace," "All," "Next," and "Quit."

10. Select one of the following:
    - Type **R** to **R**eplace the current instance and search for the next instance of the string, or
    - Type **A** to replace **A**ll instances of the string, or
    - Type **N** to skip the current instance and search for the **N**ext instance of the string, or
    - Type **Q** to **Q**uit the procedure.

STORAGE

Save File — /FS

While typing onto or editing a spreadsheet, the text typed or changes made appear on the screen and in the system's internal memory only. For that information to be permanently stored on a disk, you must use the FILE SAVE command. We strongly suggest that you save your work periodically to guard against accidental erasure.

1. Press the SLASH (/) key.

   The Main Menu will appear.

2. Type **F** to select **F**ile.

   The File Menu will appear.

3. Type **S** to select **S**ave.

   The prompt "Enter name of file to save" will appear. If the file has been saved previously, the filename and path will also appear on the prompt line.

4. Enter the name of the file to be saved:

   - If the file has *never* been saved before:

     a. Type the desired filename.

        Each filename can contain up to eight characters. Do not use spaces or the characters , ; : = ? * [ ] or / as part of the filename.

     b. Press **ENTER**.

   - If file has been saved before and you want to save ONLY the new, updated copy of the file:

     a. When the OLD filename appears, press **ENTER**.

STORAGE

A menu will appear with the selections Cancel, Replace, and Backup.

   b. Type **R** to select **R**eplace.

   The new file will replace the old copy of the file.

   NOTE: If you decide that you do not want to replace the old file with the new file, type **C** to **C**ancel the Save File command.

- If the file has been saved before and you want to save BOTH the new copy of the file AND the old copy of the file under different names:

   a. Press **BACKSPACE** or **ESC** enough times to erase the old filename.

   b. Type the NEW filename.

   c. Press **ENTER**.

- If file has been saved before and you want to save BOTH the new copy of the file AND the old copy of the file with the same name and a .BAK extension:

   a. When the OLD file name appears, press **ENTER**.

   A menu will appear with the selections Cancel, Replace, and Backup.

   b. Type **B** to select **B**ackup.

   The new file will replace the old copy of the file. The old copy of the file will be stored with the .BAK extension. To change the directory in which backups are stored, use the ? command.

   NOTE: If you decide that you do not want to replace the old file with the new file, type **C** to **C**ancel the Save File command.

NOTE: After the file is saved, a copy of the spreadsheet will remain on the screen. Use the

Worksheet Erase command (page 64) to clear the screen.

NOTE: To save a file on a disk or directory other than the default, either:

- Change the current directory before beginning the Save File command (see page 83).

OR

- Specify the new drive letter and/or directory path before typing the filename in Step 5 above.

Retrieve File — /FR

The FILE RETRIEVE command will put a copy of a worksheet file on the screen and in the system's internal memory. When a file is retrieved, any spreadsheet that is currently on the screen (and in memory) is erased.

1. Press the SLASH (/) key.

   The Main Menu will appear.

2. Type **F** to select **F**ile.

   The File Menu will appear.

3. Type **R** to select **R**etrieve.

   The prompt "Enter name of file to retrieve" will appear along with the names of the first five available files in the currently directory.

   NOTE: Press **F3** to view a screenload of available filenames.

4. Enter the name of the file to retrieve:

   a. Either **type** the name of the file or use the cursor arrow to **point to** the name of the file to be retrieved.

STORAGE

b. Press **ENTER**.

NOTE: To retrieve a file stored on a disk or directory other than the default, either:

- Change the current directory before beginning the File Retrieve command (see page 83).

OR

- Specify the new drive letter and/or directory path before typing the filename in Step 4 above.

The worksheet will be loaded into memory and a portion of it will appear on the screen.

Combine Files — /FC

The FILE COMBINE command retrieves a copy of a file from disk to memory and screen. Any file currently in memory (and on screen) remains in memory (and on screen). This allows you to combine two or more files into one worksheet.

Entries in the file that is being combined can either be COPIED, ADDED to, or SUBTRACTED from cells in the current worksheet:

- **COPY** Each entry in the file that is being combined with the current worksheet *replaces an entry* in the current worksheet

- **ADD** Only numeric data (numbers or formula results) of the file that is being combined with the current worksheet appear in the current worksheet. If the numeric data overlay a number cell or empty cell in the current worksheet, they are added to the number cell or empty cell. If the value overlays a label cell in the current worksheet, it is not added.

- **SUBTRACT** Similar to ADD except numeric data are SUBTRACTED from number cells or empty cells in the current worksheet.

To use the File Combine command, the worksheet into which entries will be added should be on the screen. See page 78 for information on retrieving files.

1. Position the pointer at the location were the combined file will appear.

2. Press the SLASH (**/**) key.

   The Main Menu will appear.

3. Type **F** to select **F**ile.

   The File Menu will appear.

4. Type **C** to select **C**ombine.

   The Combine Menu will appear.

5. Either:
   - Type **C** to select **C**opy, or
   - Type **A** to select **A**dd, or
   - Type **S** to select **S**ubtract.

   A menu will appear that allows you to combine either the Entire File or a Named Range within that file.

7. Either:
   - Type **E** to combine the **E**ntire file, or
   - Type **R** to combine a **N**amed range within the file.

   NOTE: Before combining with a named range, the range to be combined must be named (see page 108).

8. If you select Named range, the prompt "Enter range name or address" will appear:

   a. Type the range name or coordinates to be combined.

   b. Press **ENTER**.

STORAGE

The prompt "Enter name of file to combine" will appear along with the names of the first five available files in the currently directory.

NOTE: Press **F3** to view a screenload of available filenames.

9. Enter the name of the file to combine:

   a. Either **type** the name of the file or use the cursor arrow to **point** to the name of the file to be combined.

   b. Press **ENTER**.

   NOTE: To combine a file stored on a disk or directory other than the default, either:

- Change the current directory before beginning the file combine command (see page 83).

   OR

- Specify the new drive letter and/or directory path before typing the filename in Step 9 above.

Either cell A1 of the combined file or the upper left corner of the specified range within the combined file will appear at the cursor location.

NOTE: The combined file conforms to the current global formats and column widths.

File Xtract — /FX

The FILE XTRACT command allows you to save a designated range of cells as a separate worksheet file. Either the FORMULAS themselves or the current VALUES of those formulas can be extracted.

To use the File Xtract command, the worksheet that contains the cells to be extracted should be on the screen. See page 78 for information on retrieving files.

1. Press the SLASH (/) key.

   The Main Menu will appear.

2. Type **F** to select **F**ile.

   The File Menu will appear.

3. Type **X** to select **X**tract.

   The Xtract Menu will appear.

4. Either:

   - Type **F** to extract **F**ormulas, or
   - Type **V** to extract **V**alues.

   The prompt "Enter name of file to extract to" will appear along with the names of the first five files in the currently directory.

   NOTE: Press **F3** to view a screenload of filenames.

5. Enter the name under which the extracted portion of the spreadsheet will be saved:

   a. Type the desired filename.

   Each filename can contain up to eight characters. *Do not use* spaces or the characters , ; : = ? * [ ] or / as part of the filename.

   b. Press **ENTER**.

   NOTE: To extract a file to a disk or directory other than the default, either:

   - Change the current directory before beginning the file extract command (see page 83).

     OR

   - Specify the new drive letter and/or directory path before typing the filename in Step 5 above.

   The prompt "Enter extract range" will appear.

6. Point to (or type) the range to be extracted (see page 4).

STORAGE

7. Press **ENTER** to accept the range.

   NOTE: All global and range formats are saved with the extracted portion of the worksheet.

List Files — /FL

The FILE LIST command is used to display the names 1-2-3 filenames which are stored on the disk in the current drive and directory.

1. Press the SLASH (/) key.

   The Main Menu will appear.

2. Type **F** to select **F**ile.

   The File Menu will appear.

3. Type **L** to select **L**ist.

   The List Menu will appear.

4. Either:
   - Type **W** to list **W**orksheet files, or
   - Type **P** to list **P**rint files, or
   - Type **G** to list **G**raph files, or
   - Type **L** to list files **L**inked to the current worksheet, or
   - Type **O** to select **O**ther (list files of all types).

   NOTE: A copy of the listing that appears on the screen can be printed by pressing the **SHIFT + PRTSC (PRINT SCREEN)** keys.

5. Press any key to clear the listing.

File Directory — /FD

All files are saved to and retrieved from the active (current) disk drive and directory. The FILE DIREC-

TORY command will tell you which drive and directory is active and will allow you to change the active drive and/or directory. To use the FILE DIRECTORY command:

1. Press the SLASH (/) key.

   The Main Menu will appear.

2. Type **F** to select **F**ile.

   The File Menu will appear.

3. Type **D** to select **D**irectory

   The prompt "Enter current directory" will appear along with the drive letter and path of the current drive and directory. To change the active drive or directory path:

4. Type the drive and path to make it current.

   EXAMPLE: C:\LOTUS\FILES.

5. Press **ENTER**.

   NOTE: For more information about drives and paths, refer to the DOS manual that was supplied with your system.

File Erase — /FE

The FILE ERASE command will erase a worksheet, print, or graph file. Once a file is erased it can never again be edited, viewed, or printed.

1. Press the SLASH (/) key.

   The Main Menu will appear.

2. Type **F** to select **F**ile.

   The File Menu will appear.

3. Type **E** to select **E**rase.

   The Erase Menu will appear.

STORAGE

4. Either:
   - Type **W** to select a **W**orksheet file to erase, or
   - Type **P** to select a **P**rint file to erase, or
   - Type **G** to select a **G**raph file to erase, or
   - Type **O** to select **O**ther (select any type of file to erase).

   The prompt "Enter name of file to erase" will appear along with the names of the first five available files of the type specified in the currently directory.

   NOTE: Press **F3** to view a screenload of available filenames.

5. Enter the name of the file to erase:

   a. Either *type* the name of the file or use the cursor arrow to *point to* the name of the file to be erased.

   b. Press **ENTER**.

   NOTE: To erase a file stored on a disk or directory other than the default, either:

   - Change the current directory before beginning the File Erase command (see page 83).

   OR

   - Specify the new drive letter and/or directory path before typing the filename in Step 5 above.

   A menu will appear with the selections No and Yes.

6. Either:
   - Type **Y** to select **Y**es and erase the file, or
   - Type **N** to select **N**o and cancel the File Erase command.

File Import — /FI

The FILE IMPORT command is used to read text or numbers from a .PRN or other ASCII file into the current worksheet.

NOTE: A .PRN (PRINT) file is created during the print command by choosing to send a copy of the worksheet containing print specification to the FILE instead of to the PRINTER (see page 94).

The FILE IMPORT command is also used to import ASCII files created by other spreadsheet programs.

To use File Import:

1. Press the SLASH (/) key.

   The Main Menu will appear.

2. Type **F** to select **F**ile.

   The File Menu will appear.

3. Type **I** to select **I**mport.

   The Import Menu will appear.

4. Either:
   - Type **T** to select **T**ext (a maximum of 240 characters in each line in the imported file will appear as a label), or
   - Type **N** to select **N**umbers (labels and numbers from the imported file will appear in different cells on the worksheet.

   If the file being imported is not delimited, only the numbers will be imported.)

   The prompt "Enter name of file to import" will appear along with the names of the first five available files in the currently directory.

   NOTE: Press **F3** to view a screenload of available filenames.

5. Enter the name of the file to retrieve:

a. Either *type* the name of the file or use the cursor arrow to *point to* the name of the file to be imported.

b. Press **ENTER**.

NOTE: To import a file stored on a disk or directory other than the default, either:

- Change the current directory before beginning the file import command (see page 83).

OR

- Specify the new drive letter and/or directory path before typing the filename in Step 5 above.

The file will be imported and a portion of it will appear on the screen.

File Tables — /FAT

The FILE TABLES command will display a table containing the name, date, and time of creation and size (in bytes) of files saved. To produce the table:

1. Press the SLASH (/) key.

   The Main Menu will appear.

2. Type **F** to select **F**ile.

   The File Menu will appear.

3. Type **A** to select **A**dmin.

   The Administration Menu will appear.

4. Type **T** to select **T**able.

   The Table Menu will appear.

5. Select one of the following:

   - Type **W** to create a table of **W**orksheet (.WK?) files, or

   - Type **P** to create a table of **P**rint (.PRN) files, or

- Type **G** to create a table of **G**raph (.PIC) files, or
- Type **O** to select **O**ther (create a table of all files, or
- Type **L** to create a table of files **L**inked to the current spreadsheet.

    NOTE: If Linked is selected, skip to Step 7 below.

    The prompt "Enter directory" will appear along with the path to the current directory.

6. Type the name of the directory containing files to list and press **ENTER**.

    The prompt "Enter range for table" will appear.

7. Point to (or type) the range that will contain the file table.

8. Press **ENTER** to accept the range.

Linking Files

In Lotus Release 2.2, two files can be linked together. That is, the most recent (current) values that appear in specified cells of one file can automatically appear in a second file. This is done by typing the name of the file to link (the source file) within double angle brackets as part of a formula in the destination file.

For example, two files are stored on disk. The filenames are FIRST.WK1 and SECOND.WK1. FIRST.WK1 contains the value 500 in cell A1. We want that value to also appear in cell B10 of SECOND.WK1. To do this, type the following formula in cell B10 of SECOND.WK1:

+<FIRST>A1

If the value in cell A1 of FIRST.WK1 is revised and the worksheet is saved, the revised value will appear in SECOND.WK1 when it is retrieved.

If the two files are stored in different directories, the directory path can be added to the formula as part of the filename. In the example above, if FIRST.WK1 was stored in the directory C:\LOTUS\FILES, the formula would be typed:

+<C:\LOTUS\FILES\FIRST>A1

Refresh Link — /FAL

If you are working in a multiuser environment and the source file in a link is being shared, it may be necessary to use Link Refresh to update the source file value that appears in the destination file. To use the LINK REFRESH command, the destination file should be on the screen.

1. Press the SLASH (/) key.

    The Main Menu will appear.

2. Type **F** to select **F**ile.

    The File Menu will appear.

3. Type **A** to select **A**dmin.

    The Administration menu will appear.

4. Type **L** to select **L**ink-refresh.

    Linked values on the destination file will be updated.

Set File Reservation — /FAR

When working in a multiuser environment, only one user can update a file at a time. The Set File Reservation command is used to reserve the right to be the user who can update the file. The Release File Reservation command releases the file so that another user can update it. To use the FILE RESERVATION command, the file to be reserved should be on the screen.

1. Press the SLASH (**/**) key.

   The Main Menu will appear.

2. Type **F** to select **F**ile.

   The File Menu will appear.

3. Type **A** to select **A**dmin.

   The Administration menu will appear.

4. Type **R** to select **R**eservation.

   The Reservation Menu will appear.

5. Either:

   - Type **S** to select **S**et. The file reservation will be set for your workstation. You will be able to save any changes made to the file. Although other users will be able to access (view and print) the file, they will not be able to save changes as long as the reservation is set.

   NOTE: You can only do this if there is no reservation already set on that file.

   OR

   - Type **R** to select **R**elease. This will release the reservation so that another user can set a reservation and save changes to the file.

   The system will return to the Ready mode.

TRANSLATE FILES

The Lotus Translate Utility can be used to translate files from Lotus (releases 1A, 2.0, 2.01, 2.2) or Symphony (releases 1.0, 1.1, 1.2, 2.0) to either a different Lotus or Symphony release or dBase II, dBase III, or DIF format. It can also be used to translate from dBase II, dBase III, DIF, Multiplan, or VisiCalc format to any Lotus or Symphony release.

To use the Translate Utility:

1. The Access System Menu must be on the screen. If it is not,

   a. Press the SLASH (/) key.

   b. Type **Q** to select **Q**uit.

   c. Type **Y** to select **Y**es.

2. Type **T** to select **T**ranslate.

   The Translate Utility screen will appear. The prompt "What do you want to translate FROM" will also appear along with a list of file types.

3. Position the cursor over the type of file to translate FROM, and press **ENTER**.

   The prompt "What do you want to translate TO" will also appear along with a list of file types.

4. Position the cursor over the type of file to translate TO, and press **ENTER**.

   A screen will appear containing information on the criteria that the file being translated must meet. If more than one screenload of information exists, the prompt "Press ENTER to see next page" will appear at the bottom of the screen.

5. Press **ESC** after reading the translation criteria screen(s).

A screen will appear that contains the list of available files to translate FROM (source files). This list reflects files which have been located in the default drive/directory path. If you want the system to search a different drive/directory path for source files, press the **ESC** key, revise the path that appears, and press **ENTER**.

6. Position the cursor over the name of the file to translate FROM (the source file) and press **ENTER**.

    The default name for the file to translate TO (the destination file) will appear.

7. If desired, edit the name of the file to translate TO (the destination file).

8. Press **ENTER** to accept the destination file name. If you are translating from a Lotus file, a menu will appear asking whether you want to translate the entire WORKSHEET or a specified RANGE within that worksheet.

9. If your source file is in Lotus format, either:

    - Position the cursor over **WORKSHEET** then press **ENTER**. Skip to Step 10 below,

        OR

    - Position the cursor over **RANGE** and press **ENTER**. You will be prompted for the range name. Type the **NAME** of the **RANGE** to be translated and press **ENTER**.

    A menu will appear asking whether or not you want to proceed with the translation.

10. Position the cursor over **YES** and press **ENTER** to translate the file.

    After the translation is complete, the message "Translation successful" will appear.

11. Either:

- Press **ENTER** to select another file to translate using the same source and destination types. Repeat Steps 6 through 10 above,

OR

- Press **ESC** to return to first Translate Utility screen. To select additional files to translate, repeat Steps 2 through 10 above. To exit from the Translate Utility, press **ESC**. The message "Do you want to leave Translate?" will appear. Position the cursor over **YES** and press **ENTER**. The Access System Menu will reappear.

PRINTING

The Print Command — /P

The worksheet to print must be on the screen (and in memory) before the Print command can be given. For information on retrieving a worksheet, see page 78.

1. Press the SLASH (/) key.

   The Main Menu will appear.

2. Type **P** to select **P**rint.

   The Printer/File Menu will appear.

3. Either:
   - Type **P** to send output to the **P**rinter, or
   - Type **F** to send output to a **F**ile

   NOTE: If **File** is selected, the system will prompt for a filename. Type the name of the file in which the output will be stored and press **ENTER**. Files are automatically assigned a .PRN extension.

   The Print Menu and screen will appear.

4. Specify the range of cells to print:

   a. Type **R** to select **R**ange.

      The prompt "Enter print range" will appear.

   b. Point to (or type) the range of cells to be printed (see page 4).

   c. Press **ENTER** to accept the range.

5. Select the desired print options (see page 95).

6. Be sure the printer is ON and paper is loaded.

7. Be sure the paper is positioned at the top of the page. If it is not:

   a. Type **L** (**L**ine) enough times to properly position the paper, then

b. Type **A** (**A**lign) to tell the system that the spot that you have moved the paper to is the top of the page.

8. Type **G** to select **G**o.

   The specified range of cells will begin to print.

9. After all printing has been completed, type **Q** to **Q**uit the Print Menu.

   NOTE: The system retains the last set of print settings until the worksheet is erased. If you save a copy of the file after printing, the last set of print settings will be saved with the file.

Print Menu Selections

Here we provide a list of selections available on the Print Menu. See page 94 for information on using the **/Print** command to print a worksheet.

RANGE	Sets range of cells to print.
LINE	Advances paper in printer one line.
PAGE	Advances paper in printer one page.
OPTIONS	Print format options (change the appearance of printed worksheet). See below for a list of options.
CLEAR	Clears any preset print range and/or options (see page 104).
ALIGN	Aligns paper at top of page.
GO	Begins worksheet printout.
QUIT	Quits the Print Menu.

Print Options Menu Selections

Below is a list of selections available on the Print Options Menu. The Print Options Menu appears by selecting Options from the Print Menu. (See page 94 for information on using the **/P**rint command to print a worksheet.)

HEADER Standard text that appears at the top of every printed page (see page 101).
FOOTER Standard text that appears at bottom of every printed page (see page 101).
MARGINS Used to change default margin settings (see pages 97–99).
BORDERS Used to designate specific columns and/or rows to print next to the body of the spreadsheet. Allows printing of non-adjacent rows and/or columns
SETUP Specify printer setup string. This allows you to send specific commands to the printer along with the spreadsheet. This string can set print size, number of lines per inch, special print characteristics, and so on. See your printer manual for more information about setup strings. (See page 103 for an example of using a setup string.)
PG-LENGTH Used to change default page length setting (see page 100).
OTHER Control final printout format.
OTHER options:

    AS DISPLAYED Prints what is displayed on the screen — cancels CELL FORMULAS selection.

    CELL FORMULAS Prints CONTENTS of each cell (formula instead of *result* of formula) one cell per line.

    FORMATTED Prints headers, footers, page breaks, and so on.

    UNFORMATTED Prints without headers, footers, page breaks, and so on.

QUIT Quit OPTIONS Menu.

Print Default Settings

If no print options are specified, the system assumes default settings. The system default settings are:

LEFT MARGIN	4	RIGHT MARGIN	76
TOP MARGIN	2	BOTTOM MARGIN	2
PAGE LENGTH	66	SETUP STRING	none
BORDERS	none	HEADER/FOOTER	none
OUTPUT (other options)		As displayed, Formatted	

Calculating Left and Right Margins

To calculate left and right margin settings so that the spreadsheet will be centered on a printed page:

> Number of characters available per line
> <u>–Minus number of characters to be printed</u>
> Characters available for margins

LEFT MARGIN setting = one half of characters available for margins.

RIGHT MARGIN setting = number of characters in columns to be printed plus one half of characters available for margins.

EXAMPLE:

> 80 chars (available)
> <u>–60 chars (columns to be printed)</u>
> 20 chars (available for margins)

> 10 left margin (half of 20)

> 70 right margin (60 plus half of 20)

Setting Left and Right Margins — /P(P,F)OM(L,R)

To set a left or right margin:

1. The Print Options Menu must be on the screen. If it is not:

   a. Press the SLASH (/) key.

   b. Type **P** to select **P**rint.

   c. Type either **P** to send output to the **P**rinter, or **F** to send output to a **F**ile.

   d. Type **O** to select **O**ptions.

   NOTE: See page 94 for more information about the Print Command.

2. Type **M** to select **M**argins.

   The Margins Menu will appear.

3. Either:
   - Type **R** to set **R**ight margin, or
   - Type **L** to set **L**eft margin.

   The prompt "Enter right margin" or "Enter left margin" will appear.

4. Type the desired margin setting.

   Margins settings can be from 0 to 240. See page 97 for information about calculating margins.

5. Press **ENTER**.

Calculating Top and Bottom Margins

To calculate top and bottom margin settings so that the spreadsheet will be centered on a printed page:

        Total number of lines available
        Minus number of rows to be printed
        <u>–Minus six lines Header/Footer allowance*</u>
        Lines available for margins

* *NOTE:* The system allows two blank lines below the header and above the footer. It also allows one line for the header and one for the footer. (See page 101 for more information on Headers and Footers.)

TOP MARGIN setting = one half of lines available for margins.

BOTTOM MARGIN setting = one half of lines available for margins.

EXAMPLE:

    66 lines (available)
    –50 lines (rows to be printed)
    –6 lines (Header/Footer allowance)
    10 lines (available for margins)

    5 top margin (half of 10)

    5 bottom margin (half of 10)

Setting Top and Bottom Margins — /P(P,F)OM(T,B)

To set a top or bottom margin:

1. The Print Options Menu must be on the screen. If it is not:

    a. Press the SLASH (/) key.

    b. Type **P** to select **P**rint.

    c. Type either **P** to send output to the **P**rinter, or **F** to send output to a **F**ile.

    d. Type **O** to select **O**ptions.

    NOTE: See page 94 for more information about the Print Command.

2. Type **M** to select **M**argins.

    The Margins Menu will appear.

3. Either:

    - Type **T** to set **T**op margin, or
    - Type **B** to set **B**ottom margin.

The prompt "Enter top margin" or "Enter bottom margin" will appear.

4. Type the desired margin setting.

   Margins settings can be from 0 to 32. See page 99 for information about calculating margins.

5. Press **ENTER**.

Page Length — /P(P,F)OP

Lotus will allow you to vary the page length to accommodate different paper lengths and/or line spacing. To set Page Length:

1. The Print Options Menu must be on the screen. If it is not:

   a. Press the SLASH (/) key.

   b. Type **P** to select **P**rint.

   c. Type either **P** to send output to the **P**rinter, or **F** to send output to a **F**ile.

   d. Type **O** to select **O**ptions.

   NOTE: See page 94 for more information about the Print Command.

2. Type **P** to select **P**age length.

   The prompt "Enter lines per page" will appear.

3. Type the desired page length setting.

   The page length setting can be from 1 to 100 lines.

   NOTE: If your printer is set to print six lines per inch, the page length setting for standard 8½ × 11 inch paper is 66 lines (11 x 6 = 66). The page length setting for 8½ × 14 legal paper is 84 lines (14 × 6 = 84).

4. Press **ENTER**.

Page Break — /WP

The Worksheet Page command will allow you to insert a page break on any line of the worksheet. When this page break is encountered during printing, the system will end the current page and begin printing text on a new page.

To use this command:

1. Position the cursor in the row above which the page will break.
2. Press the SLASH (/) key.

    The Main Menu will appear.
3. Type **W** to select **W**orksheet.

    The Worksheet Menu will appear.
4. Type **P** to select **P**age.

    A blank row will be inserted above the cursor location. The page break symbol (::) will be appear in that row.

Header/Footer — /P(P,F)O(H,F)

The Header and Footer options allow you to type standard text that will appear at the top (HEADER) or bottom (FOOTER) of every page of the spreadsheet during printing. Both a Header and a Footer can be specified for each spreadsheet.

Header/Footer text can be left-justified, right-justified, or centered. The Header/Footer can automatically number pages and/or display current date. Headers and Footers are set by selecting HEADER or FOOTER from the OPTIONS menu.

To produce a header or footer:

1. The Print Options Menu must be on the screen. If it is not:

    a. Press the SLASH (/) key.

    b. Type **P** to select **P**rint.

    c. Type either **P** to send output to the **P**rinter, or **F** to send output to a **F**ile.

    d. Type **O** to select **O**ptions.

    NOTE: See page 94 for more information about the Print Command.

2. Either:
    - Type **H** to select **H**eader, or
    - Type **F** to select **F**ooter.

    The prompt "Enter header" or "Enter footer" will appear.

3. Type the desired Header or Footer text.

    Any or all of the following can be produced within the header/footer:

    - **PAGE NUMBER** Type the pound sign (#) at the point where you want the number to appear. During printing, the pound sign will be replaced by the proper page number.

        NOTE: If you print a second copy of the spreadsheet without quitting the Print Menu, the system will continue to sequentially number the pages starting with the last number of the previous spreadsheet. To reset the system so that the number 1 will appear on the first page of the second copy of the spreadsheet, either reset print options or quit and reissue the print command.

    - **CURRENT DATE** Type the symbol @ at the point where you want the date to appear. The format in which the date will appear is set with the **W**orksheet **G**lobal **D**efault **O**ther **C**lock command (see page 113).

- **JUSTIFICATION** Use a vertical line (uppercase backslash on most keyboards) to separate the parts of the Header or Footer that will be left-justified, centered, and right-justified.

  EXAMPLES: Left|Centered|Right

  To produce centered text only, type:

  |Centered text

  To produce centered and right justified text, type:

  |Centered text|Right-justified text

  To produce left justified and centered text, type:

  Left-justified text|Centered text

  To produce left-justified and right-justified text, type:

  Left-just text||right-just text

- **CELL CONTENTS** To use the contents of a worksheet cell as the header or footer text, type a backslash (\) and the cell address or range name of the desired cell.

4. Press **ENTER**.

   NOTE: The system reserves three lines for the header and footer: one for the text and two for separating the text from the body of the spreadsheet.

Printer Setup Strings — /P(P,F)OS

Printer Setup Strings will allow you to send specific commands to the printer along with the spreadsheet. These strings can set print size, number of lines per inch, special print characteristics, and so on.

For example, a setup string can be used to change print size to compressed. When printing with compressed print, characters are smaller (approximately 17 per inch). To set the string for compressed print:

1. The Print Options Menu must be on the screen. If it is not:

    a. Press the SLASH (/) key.

    b. Type **P** to select **P**rint.

    c. Type either **P** to send output to the **P**rinter, or **F** to send output to a **F**ile.

    d. Type **O** to select **O**ptions.

    NOTE: See page 94 for more information about the Print Command.

2. Type **S** to select **S**etup.

    The prompt "Enter setup string" will appear.

3. Type the desired setup string.

    All Printer Setup Strings begin with a backslash and contain three numbers. Setup Strings are different for every printer and can be found in your printer manual.

    EXAMPLE: \015 = compressed print on an Epson printer.

4. Press **ENTER**.

Clear Print Options — /P(P,F)C

The last set of print specifications is remembered by the system. If you save a copy of the file after printing, the last set of print specifications will be saved with the file. The Clear Print Options command can be used to clear these specifications.

To clear print options:

1. Press the SLASH (/) key.

The Main Menu will appear.

2. Type **P** to select **P**rint.

   The Printer/File Menu will appear.

3. Type either **P** to send output to the **P**rinter, or **F** to send output to a **F**ile.

   The Print Menu will appear.

4. Type **C** to select **C**lear.

   The Clear Menu will appear.

5. Either:
   - Type **A** to clear **A**ll options, or
   - Type **R** to clear any previous print **R**ange, or
   - Type **B** to clear any rows or columns that have been set to print as a **B**order, or
   - Type **F** to clear **F**ormat settings (left, right, top and bottom margins, page length and printer setup string).

   NOTE: To clear margins without clearing page length and setup string, see below.

   The specified options will be cleared.

NOTE: Some printers have small print buffers which hold specific commands to the printers. If your printer has a buffer, you may have to turn the printer off and on again to clear a previous setup string from the buffer.

Clear Margins — /P(P,F)OMN

To clear any left, right, top, and bottom margin settings:

1. The Print Options Menu must be on the screen. If it is not:

a. Press the SLASH (/) key.

   b. Type **P** to select **P**rint.

   c. Type either **P** to send output to the **P**rinter, or **F** to send output to a **F**ile.

   d. Type **O** to select **O**ptions.

   NOTE: See page 94 for more information about the Print Command.

2. Type **M** to select **M**argins.

   The Margins Menu will appear.

3. Type **N** to select **N**one.

   Left, top, and bottom margins will be reset to 0; right margins will be reset to 240.

   NOTE: To clear all formats with one command (margins, page length, and setup string), or to clear borders or print range, see page 104.

Cancel Printing — CTRL+BREAK

To Cancel Printing and stop the printer after the print command has been issued:

1. Hold the **CTRL** key.

2. Press the **BREAK** key once.

The "WAIT" mode indicator on your screen will change to "READY" and the Print Menu will disappear from the screen after cancelling the print request. If your printer continues to print, it probably has an internal buffer that needs to empty before the cancellation of the command will be recognized.

Allways Add-In

The Allways Add-In enables you to print spreadsheets

and graphs with a variety of special effects. Some of these effects are:

- A variety of fonts,
- Bold characters,
- Underlined characters (single or double underline),
- Characters printed in colors (on color printers),
- Horizontal and vertical lines,
- Boxes around cells and/or ranges of cells,
- Light, dark, or solid black shading.

To use the Allways Add-In:

1. Retrieve the spreadsheet to be printed (see page 78).
2. The Allways Add-In must be attached, either for the current work session (page 119) or as a system default (page 122).
3. The Allways Add-In must then be invoked (page 124).
4. The SLASH key (/) will display the Allways Menu. For detailed information on using the Allways Menu selections to print spreadsheets or graphs, refer to the Lotus manual that was supplied with your system.

MISCELLANEOUS

Template Construction

A template can be constructed by making the following changes to any existing spreadsheet:

- Retrieve the worksheet,
- Protect label and formula cells,
- Erase all values,
- Save template under a different filename.

Range Input — /RI

The RANGE INPUT speeds input on a template by moving the cursor to only unprotected cells when directional arrows are pressed. The **ENTER** key cancels range input. To set range input:

1. Press the SLASH (/) key.

   The Main Menu will appear.

2. Type **R** to select **R**ange.

   The Range Menu will appear.

3. Type **I** to select **I**nput.

   The prompt "Enter data input range" will appear.

4. Point to (or type) the range of cells to be included in the input range (see page 4).

5. Press **ENTER** to accept the range.

   The pointer will move to the first unprotected cell.

Range Name — /RN

It is possible to assign a NAME to a specified range of cells. If the range is named, the range name can be typed instead of the range itself whenever the system requires you to specify a range (see page 4).

MISCELLANEOUS

You MUST assign a range name before you combine a Named range in the /File Combine command (see page 83).

To assign a Range Name:

1. Position the pointer over the first cell in the range to name.

2. Press the SLASH (/) key.

   The Main Menu will appear.

3. Type **R** to select **R**ange.

   The Range Menu will appear.

4. Type **N** to select Name.

   The Name Menu will appear.

5. Select one of the following:

   - Type **C** to **C**reate or modify a range name

     The prompt "Enter name" will appear. Continue with Step 6 below.

   - Type **D** to **D**elete a range name

     The prompt "Enter name to delete" will appear. Continue with Step 6 below.

   - Type **L** to create range names from a designated range of **L**abels.

     NOTE: If you select this option, a menu will appear containing the selections Right, Down, Left, and Up. Either type R if the range to name is to the Right of the label that will become the range name, D (Down) if the range is below the label, L if the range is to the Left of the label, and U (Up) if the range is above the label. The prompt "Enter label range" will appear. Point to (or type) the range containing the range name labels, and press ENTER. (Skip Steps 6 through 9 below.)

- Type **R** to select **R**eset (delete *all* range names).

    NOTE: If you select this option, skip Steps 6 through 9 below.

6. Type the desired range name.

    A range name may be a maximum of 15 characters. Do not use spaces, commas, semicolons or, the characters + * - / & @ # or { as part of the range name.

7. Press **ENTER**.

    The prompt "Enter range" will appear.

8. Point to (or type) the range of cells to be included in the named range (see page 4).

9. Press **ENTER** to accept the range.

Range Name Table — /RNT

To produce a table (listing) of all assigned range names and their coordinates:

1. Begin the range name command:

    a. Press the SLASH (/) key.

    b. Type **R** to select **R**ange.

    c. Type **N** to select **N**ame.

    The Name Menu will appear.

2. Type **T** to select **T**able.

    The prompt "Enter range for table" will appear.

3. Point to (or type) the range that will contain the Range Name Table.

4. Press **ENTER** to accept the range.

    A list of range names and corresponding ranges will appear.

MISCELLANEOUS

Worksheet Status — /WS

The WORKSHEET STATUS command displays the following information:

- Available memory,
- Whether or not a math coprocessor is present,
- Whether or not there are any circular references,
- Recalculation method, order, and iterations (see page 111),
- Global format (see page 45),
- Global label prefix (see page 53),
- Global column width (see page 58),
- Whether global protection is on or off (see page 62),
- Whether or not zero suppression is on or off (see page 54).

To view the worksheet status:

1. Press the SLASH (/) key.

    The Main Menu will appear.

2. Press **W** to select **W**orksheet.

    The Worksheet Menu will appear.

3. Press **S** to select **S**tatus.

    The screen containing Worksheet Status will appear. After viewing this screen:

4. Press any key to continue.

    The system will return to READY mode.

Spreadsheet Recalculation — /WGR

The system usually uses NATURAL AUTOMATIC RECALCULATION. This means that the system recalculates all values on the worksheet whenever a new entry is input. When doing this, the system recalculates all formulas on which a formula depends before that formula is recalculated. However, when inputting on a large spreadsheet, this can be very time consuming. When you set Manual Recalculation, the system will only recalculate whenever the **F9** key is pressed. You can also select modes of recalculation other than Natural. To reset recalculation:

1. Press the SLASH (**/**) key.

   The Main Menu will appear.

2. Type **W** to select **W**orksheet.

   The Worksheet Menu will appear.

3. Type **G** to select **G**lobal.

   The Global Menu and Global Settings screen will appear. Current recalculation settings appear on this screen.

4. Type **R** to select **R**ecalculation.

   The Recalculation Menu will appear.

5. Either:

   - Type **M** to set **M**anual recalculation (system only recalculates when **F9** is pressed),
   - Type **A** to set **A**utomatic recalculation (system recalculates automatically),
   - Type **N** to select **N**atural recalculation (system recalculates all formulas on which each formula is dependent),
   - Type **C** to recalculate by **C**olumn,
   - Type **R** to recalculate by **R**ow,
   - Type **I** to select **I**teration (to set a specified number of recalculation passes).

MISCELLANEOUS

NOTE: If Iteration is selected, the prompt "Enter iteration count (1-50)" will appear. Type the desired number and press **ENTER**.

NOTE: If Manual is selected, the word CALC will appear in the lower right corner of the screen whenever it is necessary for you to press the **F9** key to manually recalculate the sheet. You DO NOT have to press the key every time the word CALC appears. You only have to press it when you want to see the sheet properly recalculated.

CALC Key — F9

Whenever worksheet calculation is set to manual (see above), the **F9** key can be used to recalculate all formulas.

F9 can also be used in the EDIT mode to calculate a formula and convert it to a value. For example, in the following spreadsheet:

C5:   EDIT
+A1*B1

	A	B	C	D
1	100	5		
2				

If THE **F9** (CALC) key is pressed, the value 500 will replace the formula +A1*B1 in the edit line.

Worksheet Global Defaults — /WGD

This command allows you to:

- Display current printer and directory default settings (STATUS),

- Reset printer default settings,
- Reset starting directory default (current directory when system is started),
- Enable or disable any autoexec macro,
- Reset various other defaults (international, help, clock, undo, beep, add-in).

To use any of the WORKSHEET GLOBAL DEFAULT Commands:

1. Press the SLASH (/) key.

   The Main Menu will appear

2. Type **W** to select **W**orksheet.

   The Worksheet Menu will appear.

3. Type **G** to select **G**lobal.

   The Global Menu and Global Settings screen will appear.

4. Type **D** to select **D**efault.

   The Default Menu and Default Settings screen will appear.

5. Either:
   - Type **P** to reset **P**rinter default settings (see page 97).
   - Type **D** to reset **D**irectory default settings. The prompt "Enter default directory" and the name of the current directory will appear. Type the desired directory path and press **ENTER**.
   - Type **S** to display current default **S**tatus screen.
   - Type **O** to reset **O**ther default settings (see page 117).
   - Type A to tell the system whether or not to automatically execute any Autoexec macro when the spreadsheet is retrieved (see page 160).
   - Type **U** to **U**pdate the system and save any new default settings.

MISCELLANEOUS   115

> *NOTE:* Any defaults that are changed remain in effect for the *current 1-2-3 session only* unless you select **U**pdate in Step 5 above.

Printer Defaults

To change printer defaults:

1. Follow Steps 1 through 4 on page 113.

   The Default Menu and Default Settings screen will appear.

2. Type **P** to reset **P**rinter default settings.

   The Printer Defaults Menu will appear.

3. Select the defaults to revise:

   - To revise the printer interface:

     a. Type **I** to select **I**nterface.

     b. Type either:

     1 to select first parallel port
     2 to select first serial port
     3 to select second parallel port
     4 to select second serial port
     5 to select LPT1
     6 to select LPT2
     7 to select LPT3
     8 to select LPT4

   - To specify whether or not an automatic linefeed is added to the end of each printed line:

     a. Type **A** to select **A**utoLF.

     b. Type either **Y** to select **Y**es or **N** to select **N**o.

   - To revise the default left, right, top, or bottom margin default setting:

     a. Type either:

     L to reset **L**eft margin, or

R to reset **R**ight margin, or
T to reset **T**op margin, or
B to reset **B**ottom margin.

The Prompt "Enter left margin", "Enter right margin", "Enter top margin", or "Enter bottom margin" will appear.

  b. Type the desired margin setting.

Left and right margin settings can be from 0 to 240. Top and bottom margin settings can be from 0 to 32.

  c. Press **ENTER**.

- To revise the default page length default setting:

    a. Type **P** to reset **P**age length.

    The Prompt "Enter lines per page" will appear.

    b. Type the desired page length setting.

    Setting can be from 1 to 100.

    c. Press **ENTER**.

- To specify whether or not to wait after each printed page:

    a. Type **W** to select **W**ait.

    b. Type either **Y** to select **Y**es or **N** to select **N**o.

- To revise the default printer setup string:

    a. Type **S** to reset **S**etup string.

    The Prompt "Enter setup string" will appear.

    b. Type the desired setup string.

    c. Press **ENTER**.

    NOTE: See page 103 for more information about setup strings.

- To revise the default printer:

    a. Type **N** to select **N**ame.

    A list of available printers will appear. To add

MISCELLANEOUS

printers to this list, use the Install selection from the Access System Menu.

b. Select the desired default printer.

4. Press **Q** (**Q**uit) enough times to return to the Ready mode.

NOTE: Any defaults that are changed remain in effect for the *current 1-2-3 session only* unless you select **U**pdate in Step 5 on pages 113-114.

Other Defaults

To change other defaults:

1. Follow Steps 1 through 4 on page 113.

   The Default Menu and Default Settings screen will appear.

2. Type **O** to reset **O**ther default settings.

   The Other Defaults Menu will appear.

3. Select the defaults to revise:
   - To revise international defaults:

     a. Type **I** to select **I**nternational.

        The International Menu will appear.

     b. Type either:

        P to revise **P**unctuation marks used (decimal, argument, and thousands separator), or

        C to revise the **C**urrency symbol and whether that symbol appears before or after the number, or

        D to revise the **D**ate format used for D4 (MM/DD/YY or DD/MM/YY) and D5 (DD.MM.YY or YY.MM.DD) (see page 51), or

        T to revise the **T**ime format used for D8

(HH:MM:SS or HH.MM.SS) and D9 (HH,MM,SS or HHhMMmSSs) (see page 51), or

N to revise the way in which **N**egative nubers are displayed (within parentheses or preceded by a minus sign).

c. Follow the prompts or make selections from the menus that appear.

- To specify whether or not help is instant or removable:

  a. Type **H** to select **H**elp.

  The Help Menu will appear.

  b. Type either **I** to select **I**nstant or **R** to select **R**emovable.

  NOTE: Instant is most often used on hard disk systems. *Removable* is used most often on two-disk systems. Both commands open the Help file when **F1** is pressed. However, Removable will re-close the Help file every time **ESC** is pressed to exit from a Help screen. This allows you to remove the disk that contains the Help files.

- To revise the default system clock display:

  a. Type **C** to select **C**lock.

  The Clock Menu will appear.

  b. Type either:

  S to select **S**tandard display (DD-MMM-YY and HH:MM AM/PM), or

  I to select the **I**nternational display format set (either D4 or D5), or

  N to select **N**one (date and time will not appear), or

  C to display the **C**lock (date and time), or

  F to display the current spreadsheet **F**ilename (instead of the date and time).

MISCELLANEOUS

- To specify whether the UNDO feature is active or not:

    a. Type **U** to select **U**ndo.

    b. Type either **E** to **E**nable Undo or **D** to **D**isable Undo.

    NOTE: For information on using UNDO, see page 72.

- To specify whether or not the system should beep on error:

    a. Type **B** to select **B**eep.

    b. Type either **Y** to select **Y**es or **N** to select **N**o.

- To add or detach an add-in program:

    a. Type **A** to select **A**dd-in.

    b. Type either **S** to select **S**et (specify and attach an add-in) or **C** to **C**ancel and detach an add-in.

    c. Type the name of the add-in program to set or cancel.

    d. Press **ENTER**.

4. Press **Q** (**Q**uit) enough times to return to the Ready mode.

   NOTE: Any defaults that are changed remain in effect for the *current 1-2-3 session only* unless you select **U**pdate in Step 5 on pages 113–114.

Attach Add-In — /AA

The ATTACHED ADD-IN command will add any Lotus Add-In product to memory and make it available for use by Lotus. Add-Ins *must* be attached before any of their commands can be used.

To attach an Add-In:

1. Press the SLASH (**/**) key.

   The Main Menu will appear.

2. Type **A** to select **A**dd-In.

   The Add-In Menu will appear.

3. Type **A** to select **A**ttach.

   The prompt "Enter Add-In to attach" will appear along with the names of the first five available Add-In programs.

   NOTE: If the filename of the Add-In does not appear on your disk, you will not be able to attach and use it.

4. Type or select the name of the Add-In to attach and press **ENTER**.

   A menu will appear that allows you to specify which key will be used to invoke the Add-In. (For more information about invoking the Add-In, see page 124).

5. Select one of the following:

   - Type **N** to select **N**o-Key. This will *detach* the Add-In.
   - Type **7** to use **ALT-F7** to invoke the Add-In.
   - Type **8** to use **ALT-F8** to invoke the Add-In.
   - Type **9** to use **ALT-F9** to invoke the Add-In.
   - Type **10** to use **ALT-F10** to invoke the Add-In.

   The Add-In Menu will reappear.

6. Type **Q** to **Q**uit this menu.

   NOTE: See page 124 for information on invoking (using) the Add-In. See page 122 for information on how to attach the Add-In as a default setting. See page 121 for information on detaching the Add-In.

MISCELLANEOUS

Detach Add-In — /AD

The Detach Add-In command will remove the Add-In from memory. Once the Add-In is detached, its commands can no longer be used.

To detach an Add-In:

1. Press the SLASH (/) key.

   The Main Menu will appear.

2. Type **A** to select **A**dd-In.

   The Add-In Menu will appear.

3. Type **D** to select **D**etach.

   The prompt "Select add-in to detach" will appear along with the names of any attached Add-In programs.

   NOTE: If the filename of the Add-In does not appear on your disk, you will not be able to attach and use it.

   NOTE: To detach (remove) all Add-Ins that are in memory, see below.

4. Type or select the name of the Add-In to detach and press **ENTER**.

   The Add-In Menu will reappear.

5. Type **Q** to **Q**uit this menu.

   NOTE: See page 119 for information on attaching the Add-In. See page 122 for information on how to attach the Add-In as a default setting.

Clear All Add-Ins — /AC

The CLEAR ADD-IN command will remove *all* Add-In programs from memory.

1. Press the SLASH (/) key.

   The Main Menu will appear.

2. Type **A** to select **A**dd-In.

   The Add-In Menu will appear.

3. Type **C** to select **C**lear.

   All Add-Ins will be cleared from memory and the Add-In Menu will reappear.

4. Type **Q** to **Q**uit this menu.

   NOTE: To remove a single Add-In program from memory, see page 121. See page 119 for information on attaching the Add-In. See below for information on how to attach the Add-In as a default setting.

Attach an Add-In as Default Setting — /WGDOA

This command will allow you to add or detach an Add-In as a system default.

1. Press the SLASH (/) key.

   The Main Menu will appear.

2. Type **W** to select **W**orksheet.

   The Worksheet Menu will appear.

3. Type **G** to select **G**lobal.

   The Global Menu and Global Settings screen will appear.

4. Type **D** to select **D**efault.

   The Default Menu and Default Settings screen will appear.

5. Type **O** to reset **O**ther default settings.

   The Other Defaults Menu will appear.

6. Type **A** to select **A**dd-In.

   The Add-In Menu will appear.

7. Type **S** to select **S**et (specify and attach the Add-In).

   A menu containing the numbers 1 through 8 will appear.

8. Select the number to which the Add-In will correspond.

   NOTE: Any Add-Ins already attached appear on the Default Setting Screen next to their corresponding numbers.

   The prompt "Enter name of add-in" will appear along with the names of the first five available Add-In programs.

   NOTE: If the filename of the Add-In does not appear on your disk, you will not be able to attach and use it.

9. Type or select the name of the Add-In and press **ENTER**.

   A menu will appear that allows you to specify which key will be used to invoke the Add-In. (For more information about invoking the Add-In, see page 124).

10. Select one of the following:

    - Type **N** to select **N**o-Key. This will *detach* the Add-In.
    - Type **7** to use **ALT-F7** to invoke the Add-In.
    - Type **8** to use **ALT-F8** to invoke the Add-In.
    - Type **9** to use **ALT-F9** to invoke the Add-In.
    - Type **10** to use **ALT-F10** to invoke the Add-In.

A menu will appear that allows you to specify whether or not the system will autmotically invoke the Add-In whenever 1-2-3 is started. (For more information about invoking the Add-In, see below).

11. Type either **Y** to select **Y**es (automatically invoke Add-In) or **N** to select **N**o (do not automatically invoke Add-In).

    The Add-In Menu will reappear.

12. Type **Q** to **Q**uit this menu.

    The Default Menu will reappear.

13. Type **U** to **U**pdate the system and save the new default setting.

    NOTE: To cancel the default setting, select Cancel in Step 7 above.

    NOTE: See page 119 for information on attaching the Add-In for a single session. See below for information on invoking (using) the Add-In.

Invoke Add-In — /AI or ALT+F#

The Invoke command enables the use of commands available with the specific Add-In. Before an Add-In can be invoked, it must be attached (see page 119).

To use the Invoke command:

1. Press the SLASH (**/**) key.

   The Main Menu will appear.

2. Type **A** to select **A**dd-In.

   The Add-In Menu will appear.

3. Type **I** to select **I**nvoke.

   The prompt "Enter Add-In to Invoke" will appear along with a list of the first five attached add-ins.

MISCELLANEOUS

> *NOTE:* If the name of the desired Add-In does not appear on the list, you have not attached it. See page 119 for information on how to attach the Add-In.

4. Type or select the name of the Add-In and press **ENTER**.

   The specific Add-In Menu will appear.

   NOTE: The specific Add-In Menu will also appear if you hold **ALT** and press the function key **F#** that was assigned to the Add-In during the Attach command (see page 119).

GRAPHICS GENERAL INFORMATION

Graph Command

All graphs are created, formatted, and stored from within the 1-2-3 portion of Lotus (the "1-2-3" seletion on the Access System Menu). Graphs are printed from the PrintGaph portion of the program (the "PrintGraph" selection on the Access System Menu).

Graph Menu Selections

The GRAPH command is begun by pressing the SLASH (/) key and selecting GRAPH from the Main Menu. The Graph Menu will appear. Below is a list of selections from the Graph Menu:

- **TYPE** Set the TYPE of graph (see page 132).

- **X, A THROUGH F** Specify the data to plot (see pages 129–131).

- **RESET** Reset all or some of the data plotted (see page 128).

- **VIEW** View a graph on the screen (see page 127).

- **SAVE** Save a graph on disk (see page 143).

- **OPTIONS** Set various format options (see page 134).

- **NAME** Assign a name to current graph specifications (see page 144).

- **GROUP** Specify all data ranges at once. Used when data to plot are in adjacent rows or columns within a range (see page 132).

- **QUIT** Quits the Graph Menu and returns the system to the READY mode.

Current Graph

All graph specifications that are set (type, data ranges, options, and so on) are temporarily stored in the system's memory. When the spreadsheet is saved with the **/F**ile **S**ave command (page 76), the current graph specifications are stored with the spreadsheet. If the system power goes down before the spreadsheet is saved or if the spreadsheet is abandoned, these specifications will be lost.

To save a copy of the specifications with the worksheet for later viewing or editing, you must CREATE a NAME for the graph (see page 144).

To print a graph that contains the specifications, you must SAVE the graph on disk (see page 143).

View — /GV

The VIEW command allows you to view the current graph (the graph specifications that are currently in memory). To VIEW the current graph:

1. The Graph Menu must be on the screen. If it is not:

   a. Press the SLASH (/) key.

   b. Type **G** to select **G**raph.

2. Type **V** to select **V**iew.

   The current graph will appear.

3. Press any key to clear the graph from the screen.

F10 (Graph) Key

The **F10** key will allow you to view the current graph without entering the Graph Menu. To view the current graph:

1. The system should be in the READY mode.
2. Press the **F10** key.

   The current graph will appear.
3. Press any key to clear the graph from the screen.

Reset — /GR

The RESET command will reset (delete) some or all of the current graph data plotted. To use Reset:

1. The Graph Menu must be on the screen. If it is not:

   a. Press the SLASH (**/**) key.

   b. Type **G** to select **G**.raph.
2. Type **R** to select **R**eset.

   The Reset Menu will appear.
3. Either:
   - Type **G** to reset all **G**raph settings, or
   - Type one of the letters **A** through **F** to reset data ranges **A** through F, or
   - Type **X** to reset data range **X**, or
   - Type **R** to reset all **R**anges (X, A through F, and any group range set), or
   - Type **O** to reset all **O**ptions (see page 134 for a list of options).

   The Graph Menu will reappear.

GRAPH CONSTRUCTION

BAR, STACKED-BAR, LINE Graph Construction

To construct a BAR, STACKED-BAR, or LINE graph:

1. The Graph Menu must be on the screen. If it is not:

   a. Press the SLASH (/) key.

   b. Type **G** to select **G**raph.

2. Select *Bar*, *Stacked-Bar*, or *Line* as the graph **T**ype (see page 132).

3. Specify the data to plot:
   - X-range = X-axis labels.

   Up to six sets of data can be plotted on one graph. Each range of data will appear as a separate bar or line.

   - A-range = first data-range,
   - B-range = second data-range,
   - C-range = third data-range,
   - D-range = fourth data-range,
   - E-range = fifth data-range,
   - F-range = sixth data-range.

   NOTE: If all data to plot are in adjacent rows or columns within a range, *Group* can be used to specify all data ranges at once (see page 132).

4. Set Options (see page 134)

   The following options can be set:
   - Titles (Primary, Secondary, X-axis, and Y-axis),
   - Legends,
   - Data-Labels (Line and Bar Graph only),

- Grid,
- Scale (Y-axis and Skip options only),
- Format (Line Graphs only).

5. Name and/or Save the Graph (see pages 143–144).

   NOTE: View graphs periodically to verify options and/or data range settings.

XY Graph Construction

To construct an XY Graph:

1. The Graph Menu must be on the screen. If it is not:

   a. Press the SLASH (/) key.

   b. Type **G** to select **G**raph.

2. Select *XY* as the graph **T**ype (see page 132).
3. Specify the data to plot:
   - X-range = X-axis data-range.

   Up to six sets of data can be plotted against the X-axis range. Each range of data will appear as a separate line.

   - A-range = first data-range
   - B-range = second data-range
   - C-range = third data-range
   - D-range = fourth data-range
   - E-range = fifth data-range
   - F-range = sixth data-range

     NOTE: If all data to plot are in adjacent rows or columns within a range, *Group* can be used to specify all data ranges at once (see page 132.

4. Set Options (see page 134)

    The following options can be set:
    - Titles (Primary, Secondary, X-axis, and Y-axis),
    - Legends,
    - Data-Labels,
    - Grid,
    - Scale (Y-axis, X-axis, or Skip options),
    - Format,

5. Name and/or Save the Graph (see pages 143–144).

    NOTE: View graphs periodically to verify options and/or data range settings.

PIE Chart Construction

To construct a PIE chart:

1. The Graph Menu must be on the screen. If it is not:

    a. Press the SLASH (/) key.

    b. Type **G** to select **G**raph.

2. Select *Pie* as the graph **T**ype (see page 132).
3. Specify the data to plot:
    - X-range = pie slice labels,
    - A-range = pie slice sizes.

    NOTE: If all data to plot are in adjacent rows or columns within a range, *Group* can be used to specify all data ranges at once (see page 132).

4. Set Options (see page 134).

    The following options can be set:
    - Titles (Primary and Secondary)

5. Name and/or Save the chart (see pages 143–144).

   NOTE: View charts periodically to verify options and/or data range settings.

Type — /GT

TYPE allows you to select the type of graph that will be created.

1. The Graph Menu must be on the screen. If it is not:
   a. Press the SLASH (/) key.
   b. Type **G** to select **G**raph.
2. Type **T** to select **T**ype.

   The Type Menu will appear.
3. Either:
   - Type **P** to select **P**ie, or
   - Type **L** to select **L**ine, or
   - Type **B** to select **B**ar, or
   - Type **S** to select **S**tacked-Bar, or
   - Type **X** to select **X**Y.

   The selected type will appear on the Graph Setting screen and the Graph Menu will reappear.

   NOTE: The default type is *Line*.

Group Data Range — /GG

The Group selection will allow you to specify all data ranges at once. This can be used only when data to plot are in adjacent rows or columns within a range.

GRAPH CONSTRUCTION

To specify a group data range:

1. The Graph Menu must be on the screen. If it is not:

    a. Press the SLASH (/) key.

    b. Type **G** to select **G**raph.

2. Type **G** to select **G**roup.

    The prompt "Enter group range" will appear.

3. Point to (or type) the range of cells which contain the data to be plotted (see page 4).

    A menu containing the selections Columnwise and Rowwise will appear.

4. Either:

    - Type **C** if the data to plot are arranged within **C**olumns (the first column becomes the X-range, the second column becomes the A-range, the third column becomes the B-range, and so on.), or

    - Type **R** if the data to plot are arranged within **R**ows (the first row becomes the X-range, the second row becomes the A-range, the third row becomes the B-range, and so on.)

    The ranges of plotted data will appear on the Graph Setting screen and the Graph Menu will re-appear.

GRAPH OPTIONS

Graph Options allow you to set various format options. Before any options can be set, you must select OPTIONS from the Graph Menu. The following options are available:

	Page
GRID	134
FORMAT	135
DATA LABELS	136
TITLES	137
LEGEND	138
SCALE	139
B&W	142
COLOR	142
QUIT	142

Grid — /GOG

GRID allows you to set a grid within a Line, XY, Bar, or Stacked-Bar graph. *Horizontal, Vertical* or *Both* horizontal and vertical grid lines are available. This selection will also allow you to *Clear* any grid lines which have been set.

1. The Options Menu must be on the screen. If it is not:

   a. Press the SLASH (**/**) key.

   b. Type **G** to select **G**raph.

   c. Type **O** to select **O**ptions.

2. Type **G** to select **G**rid.

   The Grid Menu will appear.

3. Either:

   • Type **H** to set **H**orizontal grid lines, or

- Type **V** to set **V**ertical grid lines, or
- Type **B** to set **B**oth horizontal and vertical grid lines, or
- Type **C** to **C**lear any existing grid lines.

The selected grid settings will appear on the Graph Setting Screen and the Options menu will reappear.

Format Graph — /GOF

Any or all data ranges on Line and XY graphs can be formatted so that they appear as *Lines* (only), *Symbols* (only), *Both* (lines and symbols), or *Neither* (lines nor symbols). To format a graph:

1. The Options Menu must be on the screen. If it is not:
   a. Press the SLASH (**/**) key.
   b. Type **G** to select **G**raph.
   c. Type **O** to select **O**ptions.
2. Type **F** to select **F**ormat.
3. Either:
   - Type **G** to format all **G**raph settings, or
   - Type one of the letters **A** through **F** to format individual data ranges **A** through **F**.
4. Either:
   - Type **L** to set format to **L**ines only, or
   - Type **S** to set format to **S**ymbols only, or
   - Type **B** to set format to **B**oth lines and symbols, or
   - Type **N** to select **N**either (clear formats).

The selected format will appear next to its data range at the bottom of the Graph Setting Screen.

5. Type **Q** to **Q**uit the Format Menu.

   The Options menu will reappear.

   NOTE: If you select neither, you will not be able to see any of the graph data unless you have set data labels (see below).

Data-labels — /GOD

DATA-LABELS are labels that appear at data points within a graph. Data-labels can be set for any or all data-ranges in Bar, XY, and Line graphs.

1. The Options Menu must be on the screen. If it is not:

   a. Press the SLASH (/) key.

   b. Type **G** to select **G**raph.

   c. Type **O** to select **O**ptions.

2. Type **D** to select **D**ata-Labels.

   The Data-Labels Menu will appear.

3. Either:
   - Type one of the letters **A** through **F** to set data labels for individual data ranges **A** through **F**, or
   - Type **G** to set data labels for the **G**roup containing all data ranges.

   The prompt "Enter data label range for first (second, third, fourth, fifth, sixth, all) data range" will appear.

4. Point to (or type) the range that will contain the data labels.

5. Press **ENTER**.

   The Position Menu will appear.

6. Either:
   - Type **C** to position the labels at the **C**enter of the data point, or
   - Type **L** to position the labels to the **L**eft of the data point, or
   - Type **A** to position the labels **A**bove the data point, or
   - Type **R** to position the labels to the **R**ight of the data point, or
   - Type **B** to position the labels **B**elow the data point.

   NOTE: In a bar graph, data labels automatically appear above positive bars and below negative bars.

   The data-label range will appear on the Graph Setting Screen and the Data Label Menu reappears.

5. Type **Q** to **Q**uit the Format Menu.

   The Options Menu will appear.

Titles — /GOT

Allows you to put titles on a graph.

1. The Options Menu must be on the screen. If it is not:

   a. Press the SLASH (/) key.

   b. Type **G** to select **G**raph.

   c. Type **O** to select **O**ptions.

2. Type **T** to select **T**itles.

   The Titles Menu will appear.

3. Either:
   - Type **F** to select **F**irst (title appears on the top line of the graph), or

- Type **S** to select **S**econd (title appears on the second line of the graph), or
- Type **X** to select **X**-axis (title appears below the horizontal axis), or
- Type **Y** to select **Y**-axis (title appears below the vertical axis).

NOTE: The X-axis and Y-axis titles appear only in bar, line, stacked-bar, and XY graphs.

4. When the prompt appears to enter the title, either:
   - Type the title, or
   - Type a BACKSLASH (\) and the coordinates of the cell containing the title.

5. Press **ENTER**.
   The title will appear on the Graph setting screen and the Options Menu will reappear.

Legend — /GOL

LEGEND allows you to set a legend for each set of bars (in a Bar or Stacked-Bar graph) or lines (in a Line or XY graph) that will identify those bars or lines.

1. The Options Menu must be on the screen. If it is not:
   a. Press the SLASH (/) key.
   b. Type **G** to select **G**raph.
   c. Type **O** to select **O**ptions.
2. Type **L** to select **L**egend.

   The Legend Menu will appear.
3. Either:
   - Type one of the letters A through F to set a legend for individual data ranges A through F, or

- Type **R** to set legends for the **R**ange containing all data.

4. When the prompt appears to enter the title, either:
   - Type the legend, or
   - Type a BACKSLASH (\) and the coordinates of the cell containing the legend, or
   - Type (or point to) the range containing the legends.

5. Press **ENTER**.

   The legend will appear on the Graph Setting screen and the Options Menu will appear.

Scale

SCALE allows you to alter the scale that the system has automatically set for the Y or X axis. The following scale options are available:

- **X-SCALE or Y-SCALE** Allows you to change the upper and lower limits of the X or Y axis. This selection also allows you to format (change the appearance of) any numbers that appear on the X or Y axis (see below).

- **SKIP** Allows you to skip selected X-axis titles at intervals. Every second, or third, or fourth (and so on.) title will appear (see page 141).

Alter X or Y Scale — /GOSX or /GOSY

This selection allows you to change the upper and lower limits of the X or Y axis. This selection also allows you to format (change the appearance of) any numbers that appear on the X or Y axis. To alter the X or Y Scale:

1. The Options Menu must be on the screen. If it is not:
   a. Press the SLASH (/) key.
   b. Type **G** to select **G**raph.
   c. Type **O** to select **O**ptions.
2. Type **S** to select **S**cale.

   The Scale Menu will appear.
3. Either:
   - Press **X** to scale the **X** axis, or
   - Press **Y** to scale the **Y** axis.

   NOTE: You will only be able to scale the X axis on XY graphs.

4. Select one of the following:
   - To manually set the upper and lower limits of the axis scale:
     a. Type **M** to select **M**anual.
     b. Type **L** to select **L**ower.
     c. Type the number that represents the desired lower limit on the scale.
     d. Press **ENTER**.
     e. Type **U** to select **U**pper.
     f. Type the number that represents the desired upper limit on the scale.
     g. Press **ENTER**.
     h. Type **Q** to **Q**uit the Scale Menu.
   - To return to AUTOMATIC scaling (system sets the upper and lower limits of the axis scale):
     a. Type **A** to select **A**utomatic.
     b. Type **Q** to **Q**uit the Scale Menu.

- To FORMAT the numbers on a scale:
    a. Type **F** to select **F**ormat.
    b. Select the desired format. (See page xx for an explanation of format settings.)
    c. If the prompt "Enter number of decimal places" appears, type the desired number of decimal places and press **ENTER**.
    d. Type **Q** to **Q**uit the Scale Menu.
- To Display or Hide the Scale Indicator:
    a. Type **I** to select **I**ndicator.
    b. Type **Y** (**Y**es) to display the indicator, or **N** (**N**o) to hide the indicator.
    c. Type **Q** to **Q**uit the Scale Menu.

The selected settings will appear on the Graph Setting Screen and the Options menu will reappear.

NOTE: Default settings are Automatic, Format General, Indicator = Yes.

Scale Skip — /GOSS

The SCALE SKIP option allows you to skip selected X-axis titles at intervals. Every second, or third, or fourth (and so on) title will appear. To skip selected titles on the X axis:

1. The Options Menu must be on the screen. If it is not:
    a. Press the SLASH (/) key.
    b. Type **G** to select **G**raph.
    c. Type **O** to select **O**ptions.
2. Type **S** to select **S**cale.

    The Scale Menu will appear.

3. Type **S** to select **S**kip.

   The prompt "Enter skip factor" will appear.

4. Type the number that represents the skip factor.

5. Press **ENTER**.

   The selected skip factor will appear on the Graph Setting Screen and the Options Menu will reappear.

   NOTE: The default setting is 1.

Black and White or Color — /GOB or /GOC

BLACK AND WHITE OR COLOR options allow you to view the graph in either black and white or color.

NOTE: The color option will only work if your hardware is configured for color graphics.

To change to black and white or color:

1. The Options Menu must be on the screen. If it is not:

   a. Press the SLASH (/) key.

   b. Type **G** to select **G**raph.

   c. Type **O** to select **O**ptions.

2. Either:
   - Type **B** select Black and white, or
   - Type **C** to select **C**olor.

   The selected setting will appear on the Graph Setting Screen and the Options Menu will reappear.

Quit — /GOQ

The Quit selection will quit the options menu and return you to the Graph Menu.

GRAPH STORAGE

General Information

All graph specifications which are set (type, data ranges, options, and so on) are temporarily stored in the system's memory. When the spreadsheet is saved with the **/F**ile **S**ave command (page 76), the current graph specifications are stored with the spreadsheet. If the system power goes down before the spreadsheet is saved or of the spreadsheet is abandoned, these specifications will be lost.

To save a copy of the specifications with the worksheet for later viewing or editing, you must CREATE a NAME for the graph (see page 144).

To print a graph that contains the specifications, you must SAVE the graph on disk (see below).

For a listing of the differences between naming and saving a graph, see page 145.

Save Graph — /GS

SAVE GRAPH allows you to save the graph that is currently in memory. Graphs must be saved before they can be printed.

1. The Graph Menu must be on the screen. If it is not:

    a. Press the SLASH (**/**) key.

    b. Type **G** to select **G**raph.

2. Type **S** to select **S**ave.

    The prompt "Enter graph filename" will appear.

3. Type the name under which you want to save the graph.

4. Press **ENTER**.

Name Graph — /GN

NAME GRAPH allows you to assign a name to the current graph specifications. These specifications are stored with the worksheet and can be recalled, viewed, or changed at any time.

1. The Graph Menu must be on the screen. If it is not:

    a. Press the SLASH (**/**) key.

    b. Type **G** to select **G**raph.

2. Type **N** to select **N**ame.

    The Name Menu will appear.

3. Select one of the following:

    - To CREATE a name for the current set of graph specifications:

        a. Type **C** to select **C**reate. The prompt "Enter graph name" will appear.

        b. Type the name under which you want to store the graph specifications.

        c. Press **ENTER**.

    - To make a named graph the current graph:

        a. Type **U** to select **U**se. The prompt "Enter name of graph to make current" along with a list of available graphs will appear.

        b. Type (or point to) the name of the graph to make current.

GRAPH STORAGE

   c. Press **ENTER**. The named graph will appear on your screen.

   d. Press any key to clear the graph.

- To DELETE a named graph:

   a. Type **D** to select **D**elete. The prompt "Enter name of graph to delete" along with a list of available graphs will appear.

   b. Type (or point to) the name of the graph to delete.

   c. Press **ENTER**.

- To delete ALL named graphs:

   Type **R** to select **R**eset.

- To produce a table of named graph information:

   a. Type **T** to select **T**able. The prompt "Enter range for table" will appear.

   b. Type (or point to) the range on the worksheet in which the table will appear.

   c. Press **ENTER**. A list of graph names, type, and titles will appear on the worksheet.

The Graph Menu will reappear.

Difference Between Graph SAVE and NAME

SAVE	NAME
Saves current graph setting on a disk.	Assigns a name to the current graph settings.
Saved graphs appear as separate files on the disk.	Named graphs are a part of the current worksheet file.

SAVE

Saved graphs can be printed.

Saved graphs cannot be viewed or changed after they are cleared from memory unless they are also named.

NAME

Named graphs cannot be printed unless they are also SAVED.

Named graphs can be viewed or changed whenever you are within the worksheet NAMED.

GRAPH PRINTING

A graph must be SAVED on disk (see page 143) before it can be printed. To print a graph:

1. The Access System Menu must be on the screen. If it is not,

    a. Press the SLASH (/) key.

    b. Type **Q** to select **Q**uit.

    c. Type **Y** to select **Y**es.

2. Type **P** to select **P**rintGraph.

    The PrintGraph Menu and screen will appear.

3. Select graphs to print (see page 149).
4. Select desired print settings (see page 149).
5. Make sure printer is ON and paper is loaded.
6. Make sure the paper is positioned at the top of the page. If it is not,

    a. Properly position the paper, then

    b. Type **A** (**A**lign) to tell the system that the paper has been moved to the top of the page.

7. Type **G** to select **G**o.

    The specified graphs will begin to print.

8. If necessary, type **P** to advance paper to top of **P**age after printing.
9. After all graphs are printed, type **E** to **E**xit to the Access System Menu.

PrintGraph Menu

The following selections can be made from the Print-Graph Menu:

- **Image-Select** Select graphs to Print (see page 149).

- **Settings** Set print options (see page 149).

- **Go** Outputs graphs to the printer.

- **Align** Set top of page.

- **Page** Advance to top of page.

- **Quit** Return to Access System Menu.

PrintGraph Screen

- **Graphs to Print** After graphs are selected they appear in this area (see page 149).

- **Size and Rotation** Default size is set. Other sizes can be set and will appear in this area (see page 150).

- **Font** Default fonts are set. Any font changes will appear in this area (see page 152).

- **Range Colors** Default colors for printer set. These can be changed if you are working on a color plotter (see page 154).

- **Hardware Settings** Default graph and font directories as well as interface and printer appear in this area. See page 155 for information on changing these settings.

- **Paper Size** The default paper size is 8.5 x 11 inches. Any changes in paper size will appear in this area (see page 157).

- **Action Settings** Defaults are set: System will not eject paper nor will it pause after printing each graph (see pages 153–154).

Selecting and Cancelling Graphs to Print

To add or remove a graph from the list of graphs to be printed:

1. The PrintGraph Menu must appear on the screen. If it does not, follow Steps 1 and 2 on page 147.

2. Type **I** to select **I**mage-select.

    A list of available graphs will appear.

3. To select or cancel selection of a graph:

    a. Use **UP ARROW**, **DOWN ARROW**, **HOME**, and/or **END** keys to position the pointer over the name of the graph to select or cancel.

    b. Press the **SPACEBAR** once. The pound sign (#) will appear before a selected graph or clear from a canceled graph.

    NOTE: The **F10** key will display a selected graph on the screen.

4. Press **ENTER** after all graphs are selected.
    The PrintGraph Menu and screen will reappear. Selected graphs will appear in the "GRAPHS TO PRINT" area.

    NOTE: To ignore all selected graphs and return to PrintGraph Menu, press **ESC** *instead of* **ENTER** in Step 4 above.

    NOTE: **F10** key will display a selected graph on the screen.

Print Settings

The SETTINGS selection of the PrintGraph Menu allows you to set any or all of the following:

IMAGE	Page
Size	150
Fonts	152
Color	154

HARDWARE	Page
Graph Directory	155
Font Directory	155
Interface	157
Printer	156
Size (length & width) of paper	157

ACTION	Page
Pause	154
Eject	153

Graph Size

GRAPH SIZE allows you to change the size of the printed graph. The default size is HALF. This means that graph will fill half the paper (roughly 6.5 x 4.5 inches). You can either set FULL size (roughly 7.0 x 9.5 inches) or manually set any other size. To change the size:

1. The PrintGraph Menu must appear on the screen. If it does not, follow Steps 1 and 2 on page 147.

2. Type **S** to select **S**ettings.

   The Settings Menu will appear.

3. Type **I** to select **I**mage.

   The Image Menu will appear.

4. Type **S** to select **S**ize.

   The Size Menu will appear.

GRAPH PRINTING   151

5. Select one of the following:
   - To set HALF size:
     a. Type **H** to select **H**alf.
     b. Type **Q** (**Q**uit) enough times to return to the PrintGraph Menu.

   - To set FULL size:
     a. Type **F** to select **F**.ull.
     b. Type **Q** (**Q**uit) enough times to return to the PrintGraph Menu.

   - To MANUALLY set size:
     a. Type **M** to select **M**anual.
     b. Type **T** to set the **T**op margin. The prompt "Enter top margin in inches" will appear.
     c. Type the desired top margin, then press **ENTER**.
     d. Type **L** to set the **L**eft margin. The prompt "Enter left margin in inches" will appear.
     e. Type the desired left margin; then press **ENTER**.
     f. Type **W** to set the graph **W**idth. The prompt "Enter width in inches" will appear.
     g. Type the desired width; then press **ENTER**.
     h. Type **H** to set the graph **H**eight. The prompt "Enter height in inches" will appear.
     i. Type the desired height; then press **ENTER**.
     j. Type **R** to set the graph **R**otation (number of degrees to turn the graph counterclockwise). The prompt "Enter rotation in degrees" will appear.
     k. Type the desired rotation; then press **ENTER**.

1. Type **Q** (**Q**uit) enough times to return to the PrintGraph Menu.

The PrintGraph Menu and screen will reappear along with selected graphs sizes.

Font

The FONT selection allows you to change the font (typeface) that appears on printed graphs. Different fonts can be set for the first (top) title and all other text on the graph. To select a font:

1. The PrintGraph Menu must appear on the screen. If it does not, follow Steps 1 and 2 on page 147.
2. Type **S** to select **S**ettings.

   The Settings Menu will appear.
3. Type **I** to select **I**mage.

   The Image Menu will appear.
4. Type **F** to select **F**ont.
5. Either:
   - Type **1** to select a font for the first title,

     OR
   - Type **2** to select a font for all the other text.

   A list of available fonts will appear.
6. Select a font:

   a. Use **UP ARROW**, **DOWN ARROW**, **HOME**, and/or **END** keys to position the pointer over the name of the font graph to select.

   b. Press the **SPACEBAR** once. The pound sign (#) will appear before a selected font.

GRAPH PRINTING

7. Press **ENTER** after font is selected.

8. Type **Q** (**Q**uit) enough times to return to the PrintGraph Menu.

   The PrintGraph Menu and screen will reappear along with selected fonts 1 and 2.

   NOTE: If no font 2 is selected, graph text will automatically use any font selected as font 1.

Eject

EJECT causes the paper to advance between graphs. It allows unattended printing with continuous form paper. To turn the Eject mode on or off:

1. The PrintGraph Menu must appear on the screen. If it does not, follow Steps 1 and 2 on page 147.

2. Type **S** to select **S**ettings.

   The Settings Menu will appear.

3. Type **A** to select **A**ction.

   The Action Menu will appear.

4. Type **E** to select **E**ject.

5. Either:
   - Type **Y** (**Y**es) to turn the eject feature on, or
   - Type **N** (**N**o) to turn the eject feature off.

6. Type **Q** (**Q**uit) enough times to return to the PrintGraph Menu.

   The PrintGraph Menu and screen will reappear along with eject status.

Pause

PAUSE causes the printer to pause after printing each graphs. To turn Pause mode on or off:

1. The PrintGraph Menu must appear on the screen. If it does not, follow Steps 1 and 2 on page 147.
2. Type **S** to select **S**ettings.

   The Settings Menu will appear.
3. Type **A** to select **A**ction.

   The Action Menu will appear.
4. Type **P** to select **P**ause.
5. Either:
   - Type **Y** (**Y**es) to turn the pause feature on, or
   - Type **N** (**N**o) to turn the pause feature off.
6. Type **Q** (**Q**uit) enough times to return to the PrintGraph Menu.

   The PrintGraph Menu and screen will reappear along with pause status.

Range Colors

Plotted data ranges can be set to print in different colors. To do this:

1. The PrintGraph Menu must appear on the screen. If it does not, follow Steps 1 and 2 on page 147.
2. Type **S** to select **S**ettings.

   The Settings Menu will appear.
3. Type **I** to select **I**mage.

   The Image Menu will appear.
4. Type **R** to select **R**ange colors.

   The Range colors Menu will appear.

GRAPH PRINTING

5. Either:
   - Type **X** to select color for **X**-range, or
   - Type one of the letters **A** through **F** to select the color for individual data ranges **A** through **F**.

   A menu containing a list of available colors will appear.

6. Select the desired color.

7. Type **Q** (**Q**uit) enough times to return to the PrintGraph Menu.

   The PrintGraph Menu and screen will reappear along with color settings.

Change Graph/Font File Directories

The system searches for graphs to print and fonts to use in the default directories. To change these directory paths:

1. The PrintGraph Menu must appear on the screen. If it does not, follow Steps 1 and 2 on page 147.

2. Type **S** to select **S**ettings.

   The Settings Menu will appear.

3. Type **H** to select **H**ardware.

   The Hardware Menu will appear.

4. Either:
   - Type **G** to revise the directory in which **G**raphs are stored, or
   - Type **F** to revise the directory in which **F**onts are stored.

   The prompt "Enter directory containing graph (.PIC) files" or "Enter directory containing font (.FNT) files" will appear along with the current directory name.

5. Type the path of the desired directory.

6. Type **Q** (**Q**uit) enough times to return to the Print-Graph Menu.

   The PrintGraph Menu and screen will reappear along with directory settings.

Select Printer

The type of printer can be changed with the PRINTER command:

1. The PrintGraph Menu must appear on the screen. If it does not, follow Steps 1 and 2 on page 147.

2. Type **S** to select **S**ettings.

   The Settings Menu will appear.

3. Type **H** to select **H**ardware.

   The Hardware Menu will appear.

4. Type **P** to select **P**rinter.

   A list of available printers appears.

5. Select a printer to use:

   a. Use **UP ARROW**, **DOWN ARROW**, **HOME**, and/or **END** keys to position the pointer over the name of the printer to select.

   b. Press the **SPACEBAR** once. The pound sign (#) will appear before a selected printer.

6. Press **ENTER** after the printer is selected.

7. Type **Q** (**Q**uit) enough times to return to the Print-Graph Menu.

   The PrintGraph Menu and screen will reappear along with the name of the selected printer.

Interface

The INTERFACE selection will allow you to specify where the device (printer) is attached.

1. The PrintGraph Menu must appear on the screen. If it does not, follow Steps 1 and 2 on page 147.

2. Type **S** to select **S**ettings.

   The Settings Menu will appear.

3. Type **H** to select **H**ardware.

   The Hardware Menu will appear.

4. Type **I** to select **I**nterface.

   A menu containing a list of available printer interfaces will appear.

5. Select the desired interface:
   - Type **1** to select first parallel port, or
   - Type **2** to select the first serial port, or
   - Type **3** to select the second parallel port, or
   - Type **4** to select the second serial port, or
   - Type **5** to select LPT1, or
   - Type **6** to select LPT2, or
   - Type **7** to select LPT3, or
   - Type **8** to select LPT4.

6. Type **Q** (**Q**uit) enough times to return to the PrintGraph Menu.

   The PrintGraph Menu and screen will reappear along with the name of the selected interface.

Paper Size

The default paper size is 8.5 x 11 inches. This can easily be changed:

1. The PrintGraph Menu must appear on the screen. If it does not, follow Steps 1 and 2 on page 147.
2. Type **S** to select **S**ettings.

    The Settings Menu will appear.
3. Type **H** to select **H**ardware.

    The Hardware Menu will appear.
4. Type **S** to select **S**ize-paper
5. Either:
    - Type **L** to revise the paper **L**ength, or
    - Type **W** to revise the paper **W**idth.

    The prompt "Enter paper length (width) in inches" will appear.
6. Type the desired length or width (in inches).
7. Press **ENTER**.
8. Type **Q** (**Q**uit) enough times to return to the PrintGraph Menu.

    The PrintGraph Menu and screen will reappear along with the selected paper size.

Reset

Once print settings have been revised (see previous pages) the RESET selection allows you to recall and reset the original settings (the default settings that were in effect at the beginning of the current PrintGraph session). To use reset:

1. The PrintGraph Menu must appear on the screen. If it does not, follow Steps 1 and 2 on page 147.
2. Type **S** to select **S**ettings.

    The Settings Menu will appear.

GRAPH PRINTING

3. Type **R** to select **R**eset.

The Printgraph Menu will reappear.

NOTE: If settings have been saved in the current session (see below), they become the default settings. In this case, the Reset command will reset the new default settings, *not* the settings which were in effect at the start of the session.

Save Settings

The SAVE selection allows you to save specified settings on the disk.

1. The PrintGraph Menu must appear on the screen. If it does not, follow Steps 1 and 2 on page 147.

2. Type **S** to select **S**ettings.

The Settings Menu will appear.

3. Type **S** to select **S**ave.

The Printgraph Menu will reappear. The settings which have been saved become the new default settings.

MACRO GENERAL INFORMATION

Command and/or text keystrokes can be stored by the system. Each collection of keystrokes is stored on the disk under a unique *Macro Name* (also called *Macro Label*). These keystrokes can be recalled by holding the **ALT** key and typing the Macro Name, or by pressing the RUN keys (**ALT+F3**) and typing the Macro Name.

Macros eliminate unnecessary repetitive typing. Almost anything that can be done from the keyboard can be done with a macro. For example:

- Set standard specifications,
- Input labels,
- Set formats,
- Construct custom menus.

Automatic Execution

Any filename AUTO123 that is stored in the default directory will automatically load whenever 123 is entered from the Access System Menu.

Any macro named \0 (the number zero) will automatically execute whenever the spreadsheet containing that macro is retrieved if the **/W**orksheet **G**lobal **D**efault **A**utoexec is set to **Y**es (see below).

Set Autoexec as a Default — /WGDA

Any macro named \0 (the number zero) will automatically execute whenever the spreadsheet containing that macro is retrieved if the Autoexec default is set to yes. To turn this feature on or off:

MACRO GENERAL INFORMATION

1. Press the SLASH (/) key.

    The Main Menu will appear.

2. Type **W** to select **W**orksheet.

    The Worksheet Menu will appear.

3. Type **G** to select **G**lobal.

    The Global Menu and Global Settings screen will appear.

4. Type **D** to select **D**efault.

    The Default Menu and Default Settings screen will appear.

5. Type **A** to select **A**utoexec.

6. Tell the system whether or not to automatically execute any /0 macro when the spreadsheet is retrieved, either:

    - Type **Y** to select **Y**es, or
    - Type **N** to select **N**o.

    The Default Menu will reappear.

7. Type **U** to **U**pdate the system and save the new default settings.

Step Execution — ALT+F2

STEP EXECUTION allows the user to view the operation of macro in detail and facilitates debugging procedure. It tells the macro to execute one Step at a time. To use step execution:

1. Press **ALT+F2** before executing the macro.

2. Run the desired macro:
    - If the macro name is a backslash and a one-character label, hold **ALT** and type the **Macro Label**.

- If the macro name is either a backslash and a one-character label or a label of up to 15 characters, press **ALT+F3**, then type or point to the name of the macro, and press **ENTER**.

Whenever ANY KEY is pressed, the next step of the macro will be executed.

NOTE: If an error is encountered, **CTRL+BREAK** can be used to end macro execution.

3. Press **ALT+F2** to turn off step execution.

PLANNING AND CONSTRUCTING MACROS

Steps in Macro Construction

To construct macros:

1. Perform the desired operation at the keyboard. Write down the keystrokes.
2. Assign and type the Macro Label (see page 164).
3. Type the keystrokes which will be recalled when the macro the executes. Annotate those keystrokes (see page 167).
4. Assign a Range Name to the Macro (see page 167).
5. Save a copy of the file.

Placement of Macro Parts

The diagram below illustrates the placement of the parts of a macro.

	AA	AB	AD
100	Macro Label	Starting cell	Annotation
101		Keystrokes	Annotation
102		Keystrokes	Annotation
103		Keystrokes	Annotation

In this example, the Macro Label is placed in cell AA100.

The first macro keystrokes are typed in the *starting cell (AB100)*, that is to the right of the macro label. Subsequent *keystrokes* appear below and adjacent to the starting cell (AB101 through AB103).

Annotation for each set of keystrokes appears next to the cell containing those keystrokes. Annotation could have appeared in ANY column. In this example, we used column AD to allow enough room for display of the macro keystrokes in column AB.

All macros should be placed somewhere on the worksheet where they will not be affected by changes to the data. Lotus suggests that they be placed below and to the right of the data.

If the macros will be used with several different worksheets, they can be saved in a separate macro file. You can then use the Macro Library Manager Add-In to use these macros. See page 172 for more information about the Macro Library Manager.

Macro Label

Macro labels can be constructed in one of two ways. Either:

1. **BACKSLASH** and any **LETTER** from A through Z. The identifying **LETTER** will be used to recall (use) the macro.

    When typing this type of Macro Label on the worksheet, the first character typed must be a Label Prefix (see page 21). If the Label Prefix is not used, the Macro Label will appear as a Repeating Label. A macro with this type of label can be recalled by holding the **ALT** key and typing the Macro Name, or by pressing the RUN keys (**ALT+F3**) and typing the Macro Name.

2. Any name up to 15 characters.

    A macro with this type of label can be recalled by pressing the RUN keys (**ALT+F3**) and typing the Macro Name.

PLANNING AND CONSTRUCTING MACROS

NOTE: The name may not contain spaces, commas, semicolons, or the characters + * - / & @ # or {.

NOTE: A **BACKSLASH** and the number ZERO (**\0**) can be used as a macro label for an autoexecute macro (see page 160). Any macro with this label can not be recalled from the keyboard with **ALT+0**, but it can be recalled by pressing the RUN keys (**ALT+F3**) and typing **0**.

NOTE: The macro label does **not have to be typed on** the worksheet. However when a macro label appears on the screen, the macro will be more easily identified and you will be able to use the RANGE NAME LABEL RIGHT command to name the range (see page 167).

Typing Macro Keystrokes

Macro keystrokes must be stored within cells as *Label* entries. If necessary, a label prefix should be used (see page 21).

It is suggested that the first cell to contain keystrokes (the STARTING CELL) should be directly to the right of the cell containing the Macro Label. The **/R**ange **N**ame **L**abel **R**ight command can then be used to name a range of macro labels (see page 167).

Macro keystrokes can be stored in one or more cells. Subsequent cells used should be adjacent to and below the STARTING CELL (see the diagram on page 163). The system will continue reading keystrokes until it encounters a blank cell.

While typing macro keystrokes, any letter, word, number, or function can be included. *Functions* which are being included must be written out and appear within brackets (see page 166). The **ENTER** keystroke should be typed as a tilde (~).

Function Keys used in Macros

Function	Should Be Typed
HOME	{HOME}
END	{END}
PAGE UP	{PGUP}
PAGE DOWN	{PGDN}
BACKSPACE	{BACKSPACE} or {BS}
UP ARROW	{UP} or {U}
DOWN ARROW	{DOWN} or {D}
RIGHT ARROW	{RIGHT} or {R}
LEFT ARROW	{LEFT} or {L}
CTRL+RIGHT ARROW	{BIGRIGHT}
CTRL+LEFT ARROW	{BIGLEFT}
TAB	{BIGRIGHT}
BACKTAB (SHIFT+TAB)	{BIGLEFT}
DEL	{DELETE} or {DEL}
INS	{INSERT} or {INS}
ESC	{ESCAPE} or {ESC}
F1	{HELP}
F2	{EDIT}
F3	{NAME}
F4	{ABS}
F5	{GOTO}
F6	{WINDOW}
F7	{QUERY}
F8	{TABLE}
F9	{CALC}
F10	{GRAPH}
ALT+F7	{APP1}
ALT+F8	{APP2}
ALT+F9	{APP3}
ALT+F10	{APP4}
/ (slash)	/ or or {MENU}
~ (tilde)	{~}
{ (open brace)	{{}
} (close brace)	{}}

Macro Annotation

Macro annotations are descriptive notes typed next to macro keystroke entries. They are helpful when working with complex macros or when returning to macros at a later time.

The macro annotation is not absolutely necessary for operating the macro. However, a macro without annotation **will be more difficult to read and understand**.

Assigning a Macro Label — /RN

The **RANGE NAME** command is used to assign a Macro Label. The NAME is the Macro Label. The RANGE is the first cell containing macro keystrokes (the *Starting Cell*).

If the Macro starting cell appears in the cell directly to the right of the Macro Label, the **/R**ange **N**ame **L**abel **R**ight command can be used. To use this command:

1. Position the pointer over the macro label to be named.

2. Press the SLASH (/) key.

   The Main Menu will appear.

3. Type **R** to select **R**ange.

   The Range Menu will appear.

4. Type **N** to select **N**ame.

   The Name Menu will appear.

5. Type **L** to select **L**abel.

   A menu will appear containing the selections Right, Down, Left, and Up.

6. Since the starting cell is to the **R**ight of the label, type **R** to select **R**ight.

   The prompt "Enter label range" will appear.

7. Point to (or type) the range containing the macro labels.

8. Press **ENTER** to accept the range.

If the macro label does **not appear on the** worksheet or if the Macro Starting Cell does not appear in the cell directly to the right of the Macro Label, the **/R**ange **N**ame **C**reate command can be used. To use this command:

1. Position the pointer over the macro starting cell.

2. Press the SLASH (**/**) key.

   The Main Menu will appear.

3. Type **R** to select **R**ange.

   The Range Menu will appear.

4. Type **N** to select **N**ame.

   The Name Menu will appear.

5. Type **C** to select **C**reate range name.

   The prompt "Enter name" will appear.

6. Type the desired macro label name.

   Since a macro label is a range name, it may be a maximum of 15 characters. Do not use spaces, commas, semicolons, or the characters + * - / & @ # or { as part of the macro label name.

7. Press **ENTER**.

   The prompt "Enter range" will appear. Only the starting cell needs to be named.

8. Since the cursor is already positioned over this cell, press **ENTER** to accept the range.

Run (Use) Macro — ALT+F3

Each collection of macro keystrokes is stored on the disk under a unique *Macro Name* (also called *Macro Label*). These keystrokes can be recalled by holding the **ALT** key and typing the Macro Name (if the macro name is a slash and a single character), or by using the RUN keys (**ALT+F3**). To use **ALT+F3**:

1. Hold **ALT** and press **F3**.

    The prompt "Select the macro to run" will appear along with a list of available macro names.

2. Point to (or type) the name of the macro to run.

3. Press **ENTER** to accept the name.

    The macro will run.

MACRO LIBRARY MANAGER

General Information

If macros will be used with several different worksheets, they can be saved in a separate macro file. You can then use the Macro Library Manager Add-In to use these macros with any worksheet.

To use the Macro Library Manager:

1. Create, label, and name the macros which will be contained in the library (see page 163).

2. Save these macros to a macro file (see pages 176–177).

3. To use the macros, the Library Manager must be attached, either for the current work session below or as a system default (page 173).

4. The Library Manager must then be invoked (page 119) and the specific macro file to be used must be loaded into memory (page 175).

5. Macros that are contained in this file can then be run (see page 169).

Attach Library Manager Add-In — /AA

The Attach Add-In command will add the Macro Library Manager to memory and make it available for use by Lotus. This Library Manager *must* be attached before any Library commands can be used.

To attach the Library Manager Add-In:

1. Press the SLASH (/) key.

    The Main Menu will appear.

MACRO LIBRARY MANAGER

2. Type **A** to select **A**dd-In.

   The Add-In Menu will appear.

3. Type **A** to select **A**ttach.

   The prompt "Enter Add-In to attach" will appear along with the names of the first five available Add-In programs.

   NOTE: The name of the Macro Library Manager file is MACROMGR.ADN. If that filename does not appear on your disk, you will not be able to attach and use the Library Manager.

4. Type or select MACROMGR and press **ENTER**.

   A menu will appear that will allow you to specify which key will be used to invoke the Add-In. (For more information about invoking the Add-In, see page 175.)

5. Select one of the following:

   - Type **N** to select **N**o-Key. This will *detach* the Library Manager.
   - Type **7** to use **ALT+F7** to invoke the Library Manager.
   - Type **8** to use **ALT+F8** to invoke the Library Manager.
   - Type **9** to use **ALT+F9** to invoke the Library Manager.
   - Type **10** to use **ALT+F10** to invoke the Library Manager.

   The Add-In Menu will reappear.

6. Type **Q** to **Q**uit this menu.

   NOTE: See page 175 for information on invoking (using) the Add-In. See page 173 for information on how to attach the Add-In as a default setting. See page 172 for information on detaching the Add-In.

Detach Library Manager Add-In — /AD

The Detach Add-In command will remove the Macro Library Manager from memory. Once the Library Manager is detached, Library commands can no longer be used.

To detach the Library Manager Add-In:

1. Press the SLASH (/) key.

   The Main Menu will appear.

2. Type **A** to select **A**dd-In.

   The Add-In Menu will appear.

3. Type **D** to select **D**etach.

   The prompt "Select Add-In to detach" will appear along with the names of any attached Add-In programs.

   NOTE: The name of the Macro Library Manager file is MACROMGR.ADN. If that filename does not appear on the list, the Library Manager is not currently attached.

   NOTE: To detach (remove) all Add-Ins that are in memory, see below.

4. Type or select MACROMGR and press **ENTER**.

   The Add-In Menu will reappear.

5. Type **Q** to **Q**uit this menu.

   NOTE: See page 170 for information on attaching the Add-In. See page 173 for information on how to attach the Add-In as a default setting.

Clear All Add-Ins — /AC

The CLEAR ALL ADD-IN command will remove *all* add-in programs from memory.

1. Press the SLASH (/) key.

   The Main Menu will appear.

2. Type **A** to select **A**dd-In.

   The Add-In Menu will appear.

3. Type **C** to select **C**lear.

   All Add-Ins will be cleared from memory and the Add-In Menu will reappear.

4. Type **Q** to **Q**uit this menu.

   NOTE: To remove a single Add-In program from memory, see page 172. See page 170 for information on attaching the Add-In. See below for information on how to attach the Add-In as a default setting.

Attach Library Manager Add-In as Default Setting — /WGDOA

The ATTACH LIBRARY MANAGER ADD-IN AS DEFAULT SETTING command allows you to add or detach the Macro Library Manager Add-In as a system default.

1. Press the SLASH (/) key.

   The Main Menu will appear

2. Type **W** to select **W**orksheet.

   The Worksheet Menu will appear.

3. Type **G** to select **G**lobal.

   The Global Menu and Global Settings screen will appear.

4. Type **D** to select **D**efault.

The Default Menu and Default Settings screen will appear.

5. Type **O** to reset **O**ther default settings.

    The Other Defaults Menu will appear.

6. Type **A** to select **A**dd-In.

    The Add-In Menu will appear.

7. Type **S** to select **S**et (specify and attach the Add-In).

    A menu containing the numbers 1 through 8 will appear.

8. Select the number to which the Library Manager corresponds.

    NOTE: Any Add-Ins already attached appear on the Default Setting Screen next to their corresponding numbers.

    The prompt "Enter name of Add-In" will appear along with the names of the first five available Add-In programs.

    NOTE: The name of the Macro Library Manager file is MACROMGR.ADN. If that filename does not appear on your disk, you will not be able to attach and use the Library Manager.

9. Type or select MACROMGR and press **ENTER**.

    A menu will appear that allows you to specify which key will be used to invoke the Add-In. (For more information about invoking the Add-In, see page 175.)

10. Select one of the following:

    - Type **N** to select **N**o-Key. This will *detach* the Library Manager.
    - Type **7** to use **ALT+F7** to invoke the Library Manager.

MACRO LIBRARY MANAGER

- Type **8** to use **ALT+F8** to invoke the Library Manager.
- Type **9** to use **ALT+F9** to invoke the Library Manager.
- Type **10** to use **ALT+F10** to invoke the Library Manager.

A menu will appear which will allow you to specify whether or not the system will automatically invoke the Library Manager whenever 1-2-3 is started. (For more information about invoking the add-in, see below.)

11. Type either **Y** to select **Y**es (automatically invoke Add-In) or **N** to select No (do not automatically invoke Add-In).

    The Add-In Menu will reappear.

12. Type **Q** to **Q**uit this menu.

    The Default Menu will reappear.

13. Type **U** to **U**pdate the system and save the new default setting.

    NOTE: To cancel the default setting, select Cancel in Step 7 above.

    NOTE: See page 170 for information on attaching the Add-In for a single session. See below for information on invoking (using) the Add-In.

Invoke Library Manager Add-In — /AI or ALT+F#

The INVOKE command is used to load or remove an Add-In from memory, to save or edit macros in a library file, or list range names in a library file.

Before a library file can be invoked, the Library Manager Add-In must be attached (see page 170).

To use the Invoke command:

1. Press the SLASH (/) key.

   The Main Menu will appear.

2. Type **A** to select **A**dd-In.

   The Add-In Menu will appear.

3. Type **I** to select **I**nvoke.

   The prompt "Enter Add-In to invoke" will appear along with a list of the first five attached Add-Ins.

   NOTE: The name of the Macro Library Manager file is MACROMGR. If that file name does not appear on the list, you have not attached it. See page 170 for information on how to attach the Add-In.

4. Type or select MACROMGR and press **ENTER**.

   The Library Add-In Menu will appear with the following choices:

Load	Used to bring a copy of the specified library file into memory so that the macros from that file can be used. See page 180 for more information.
Save	Used to save defined macros in a library file. See page 177 for more information.
Edit	Allows you to edit macros that are stored in a library file. See page 178 for more information.
Remove	Used to clear a library file from memory. See page 181 for more information.
Name-List	Creates a list of the range names that are contained in the library file that is currently in memory. See page 181 for more information.

NOTE: The above Library Add-In Menu will also appear if you hold **ALT** and press the function key that was assigned to the Library Manager during the Attach command (see page 170).

Save Library File — /AIS

The SAVE LIBRARY FILE command is used to save defined macros in a library file for later reuse.

To save a library file, the macros to be saved must appear on the current worksheet, the macro label must be defined for all macros which will be retrieved (see page 163), and the Invoke Add-In Menu must be on the screen:

1. Either:
   - Hold **ALT** and press the function key that was assigned to the Library Manager during the Attach command (see page 170), or
   - Type **/AI** (SLASH, **A**dd-in, **I**nvoke).

   The Invoke Add-In Menu will appear.

2. Type **S** to select **S**ave.

   The prompt "Enter name of macro library to save" will appear.

3. Enter the name of the library:

   a. Type the desired filename.

   Each filename can contain 8 characters. *Do not use* spaces or the characters , ; : = ? * [ ] or / as part of the filename.

   b. Press **ENTER** to accept the name.

   NOTE: All library files will automatically be assigned an .MLB extension by the system.

If a library file has already been saved under the specified name, a menu will appear that will ask if you want to overwrite that file. Type either **Y** (**Y**es) if you do want to overwrite the file, or **N** (**N**o) if you do not want to overwrite the file.

The prompt: "Enter macro library range" will appear.

4. Point to (or type) the range that contains the macros to be saved (see page 4).

A menu will appear that will ask if you want to use a password to lock the library. If you do lock the library, no one will be able to edit its contents without the password.

5. Decide whether or not to lock the library:

- Type **N** (**N**o) if you do not want to lock the file, or
- Type **Y** (**Y**es) if you do want to lock the file.

The system will prompt "Enter password". Type the password and press **ENTER**. If you forget this password, you will never be able to edit the library file.

The file will be saved and the macros that appeared in the specified range will be cleared from the screen.

Edit Library File — /AIE

This command is used to edit macros which have previously been saved in a library file.

To edit a library file the library file must first be loaded into memory (see page 180) and the Invoke Add-In Menu must be on the screen:

1. Either:
   - Hold **ALT** and press the function key that was assigned to the Library Manager during the Attach command (see page 170), or

MACRO LIBRARY MANAGER

- Type **/AI** (SLASH, **A**dd-in, **I**nvoke).

   The Invoke Add-In Menu will appear.

2. Type **E** to select **E**dit.

   The prompt "Enter name of macro library to edit" will appear along with the name of the library file currently in memory.

3. Enter the name of the library file to edit:

   a. Either **type** the name of the file or use the cursor arrow to **point to** the name of the file to be edited.

   b. Press **ENTER**.

   If the library file had been locked with a password, the prompt "Enter password" will appear.

4. If necessary, type the password and press **ENTER**.

   A menu will appear that will allow you to tell the system to either **Ignore** any range name in the library file that conflicts with a range name that is in the current worksheet file, or **Overwrite** any range name in the worksheet with a conflicting name in the library file.

5. Either:

   - Type **I** to **I**gnore conflicting range names, or
   - Type **O** to **O**verwrite a conflicting worksheet range names with library range names.

   The prompt "Enter range for macro library" will appear.

6. Type (or point to) the range on the worksheet where macros from the library file will appear.

7. Press **ENTER** to accept the range.

   The macros from the library file will appear on the worksheet. These macros can now be edited and re-saved on the library file (see page 177.)

Load Library File — /AIL

The LOAD LIBRARY FILE command is used to bring a copy of the specified library file into memory so that the macros from that file can be used.

To load a library file, the Invoke Add-In Menu must be on the screen:

1. Either:

    - Hold **ALT** and press the function key that was assigned to the Library Manager during the Attach command (see page 170), or

    - Type **/AI** (SLASH, **A**dd-in, **I**nvoke).

    The Invoke Add-In Menu will appear.

2. Type **L** to select **L**oad.

    The prompt "Enter name of macro library to load" will appear along with a list of available library files.

    NOTE: All library files have an .MLB extension.

3. Enter the name of the library file to load:

    a. Either **type** the name of the file or use the cursor arrow to **point to** the name of the file to be loaded.

    b. Press **ENTER**.

    If a library file is already loaded into memory, a menu will appear that will ask if you want to overwrite that file. Type either **Y** (**Y**es) if you want to overwrite the file, or **N** (**N**o) if you do not want to overwrite the file.

    The Invoke Add-In Menu will reappear on the screen.

4. Type **Q** to **Q**uit this menu.

Remove Library File — /AIR

The REMOVE LIBRARY FILE command is used to remove the current library file from memory.

To remove a library file, the Invoke Add-In Menu must be on the screen:

1. Either:
    - Hold **ALT** and press the function key that was assigned to the Library Manager during the Attach command (see page 170), or
    - Type **/AI** (SLASH, **A**dd-in, **I**nvoke).

    The Invoke Add-In Menu will appear.

2. Type **R** to select **R**emove.

    The prompt "Enter name of macro library to remove" will appear along with the name of the library file currently in memory.

3. Enter the name of the library file to remove:

    a. Either **type** the name of the file or use the cursor arrow to **point to** the name of the file to be removed.

    b. Press **ENTER**.

    The Invoke Add-In Menu will be cleared from the screen.

List the Names of Macros in Current Library File — /AIN

This command is used to create a list of the range names (macro labels) which are contained in the library file that is currently in memory.

To create a list of range names, the Invoke Add-In Menu must be on the screen:

1. Either:
   - Hold **ALT** and press the function key that was assigned to the Library Manager during the Attach command (see page 170), or
   - Type **/AI** (SLASH, **A**dd-in, **I**nvoke).

   The Invoke Add-In Menu will appear.

2. Type **N** to select **N**ame-List.

   The prompt "Enter name of macro library name" will appear along with the name of the library file currently in memory.

3. Enter the name of the library file in memory:
   a. Either **type** the name of the file or use the cursor arrow to **point to** the name of the file to be removed.
   b. Press **ENTER**.

   The prompt "Enter range for list" will appear.

4. Point to (or type) the range on the worksheet in which the list of names will appear (see page 4).

5. Press **ENTER** to accept the range.

   The list of macro label names will appear in the specified range and the Invoke Add-In Menu will be cleared from the screen.

LEARN

General Information

The Learn feature will allow you to designate an area on the worksheet where macros keystrokes will automatically appear as you type the corresponding commands from the keyboard. The following steps are involved in using Learn:

1. Designate a Learn Range (see below).
2. Turn on the Learn feature (see page 184).
3. Perform the actions at the keyboard which you want recorded as macro keystrokes.
4. Turn off the Learn feature.
5. Label and annotate the keystrokes which have been recorded (see page 167).

Specifying a Learn Range — /WLR

The Learn Range is the area in which macro keystrokes will appear.

1. Press the SLASH (/) key.

    The Main Menu will appear.

2. Type **W** to select **W**orksheet.

    The Worksheet Menu will appear.

3. Type **L** to select **L**earn.

    The Learn Menu will appear.

4. Type **R** to select **R**ange.

    The prompt "Enter learn range" will appear.

5. Type (or point to) the range that will contain the recorded macro keystrokes.

   NOTE: The range should be within a single column, but should be large enough to contain the keystrokes to be recorded.

6. Press **ENTER** to accept the range.

   NOTE: For information on recording keystrokes, see below.

Recording Macro Keystrokes — ALT+F5

To use the Learn feature to record keystrokes, a learn range must first be specified (see page 183). After the learn range has been specified:

1. Hold **ALT** and press **F5** to turn on the Learn feature.

   The LEARN indicator will appear at the bottom of the screen.

2. Perform the keyboard actions that you want recorded as macro keystrokes.

   After all keystrokes have been performed,

3. Hold **ALT** and press **F5** to turn off the Learn feature.

   NOTE: Keystrokes that have been recorded with the learn feature will not have macro labels or annotations. These will have to be added. See page 167 for information on macros labels. See page 167 for information on annotation.

LEARN

Cancel Learn Range — /WLC

To cancel a learn range:

1. Press the SLASH (/) key.

   The Main Menu will appear.

2. Type **W** to select **W**orksheet.

   The Worksheet Menu will appear.

3. Type **L** to select **L**earn.

   The Learn Menu will appear.

4. Type **C** to select **C**ancel.

   The range will be cancelled and the Learn Menu will disappear from the screen.

Erase Contents of Learn Range — /WLE

The Erase contents of learn range command will erase any macro keystrokes which have been recorded and stored in a learn range (see page 184).

1. Press the SLASH (/) key.

   The Main Menu will appear.

2. Type **W** to select **W**orksheet.

   The Worksheet Menu will appear.

3. Type **L** to select **L**earn.

   The Learn Menu will appear.

4. Type **E** to select **E**rase.

   The contents of the range will be erased and the Learn Menu will disappear from the screen.

   NOTE: The Learn range will not be cancelled. To cancel a Learn range, see above.

/X MACRO COMMANDS

/X Commands

The /X commands are a group of commands which can only be written into macros; they CANNOT be invoked from the keyboard. These command keystrokes are stored within cells as LABEL entries. More information about the /X commands can be found on the following pages:

/XL (pause for label input)	203
/XN (pause for numeric input)	204
/XI (if/then)	197
/XQ (quit macro)	202
/XM (macro menu)	199
/XG (go to macro)	193
/XC (call macro)	192
/XR (return from macro)	193

All Lotus releases (1A, 2, 2.2, 3) can use the /X commands. However, all releases, *except* 1A, also use an enhanced format for these commands. They are as follows:

All Releases	All Releases Except 1A
/XL	{GETLABEL}
/XN	{GETNUMBER}
/XI	{IF}
/XQ	{QUIT}
/XM	{MENUBRANCH}
/XG	{BRANCH}
/XC	{MENUCALL} or subroutine
/XR	{RETURN}

If you are going to be using macros which will be transported to version 1A, use only the /X macro commands.

Advanced Macro Commands

Advanced macro commands have been grouped by category. More information on these commands can be found on the pages listed below:

LOOPING AND CALLING Commands (redirect the flow of macro keystroke execution)

	Page
{subroutine}	191
{BRANCH}	193
{DEFINE}	194
{DISPATCH}	194
{FOR}	196
{FORBREAK}	196
{IF}	197
{ONERROR}	195
{RESTART}	195
{RETURN}	193
{SYSTEM}	198

USER-DEFINED MENU Commands (allow the construction, display, and use of custom menus)

	Page
{MENUBRANCH}	199
{MENUCALL}	200

MACRO SUSPENSION Commands (pause or susend macro execution)

	Page
{BREAK}	202
{QUIT}	202
{WAIT}	202

USER-INPUT Commands (pause macro execution and accept keyboard input from the user)

	Page
{?}	203
{GET}	203
{GETLABEL}	203
{GETNUMBER}	204
{LOOK}	205

SPREADSHEET MANIPULATION Commands (manipulate the contents of cells on a spreadsheet)

	Page
{BLANK}	206
{CONTENTS}	206
{LET}	207
{PUT}	208
{RECALC}	208
{RECALCCOL}	209

ENVIRONMENT Commands (control the Lotus 1-2-3 environment during macro execution)

	Page
{BEEP}	210
{BORDERSOFF}	210
{BORDERSON}	210
{BREAKOFF}	210

{BREAKON}	210
{FRAMEOFF}	210
{FRAMEON}	210
{GRAPHOFF}	210
{GRAPHON}	210
{INDICATE}	211
{PANELOFF}	211
{PANELON}	211
{WINDOWSOFF}	212
{WINDOWSON}	212

TEXT FILE MANIPULATION   Commands (allow the systemto write to and read from an external ASCII file)

	Page
{CLOSE}	214
{FILESIZE}	215
{GETPOS}	216
{OPEN}	213
{READ}	214
{READLN}	214
{SETPOS}	216
{WRITE}	215
{WRITELN}	215

LOOPING AND CALLING

Comparison of /XC, {subroutine}, /XG, {BRANCH}, and {DISPATCH}

All of these commands instruct the system to go to another cell and execute keystrokes. However, the /XC and {subroutine} commands tell the system that it will eventually return to main (calling) macro. This will happen whenever the system encounters the /XR or {RETURN} command keystrokes. The system *does not return to main macro* when /XG, {BRANCH}, or {DISPATCH} command is used.

The /XC command:

MAIN MACRO   NEW MACRO

keystrokes   ➤ keystrokes
keystrokes   keystrokes
/XCnewmacro~   keystrokes
keystrokes ◀───────────────── /XR~

The {subroutine} command:

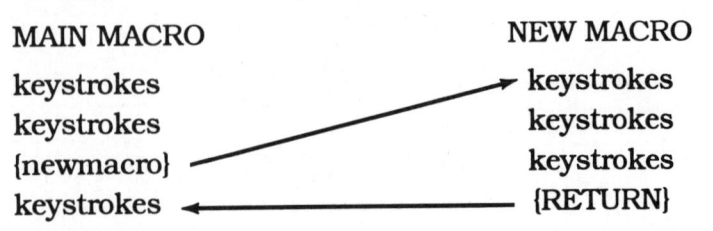

MAIN MACRO   NEW MACRO

keystrokes   ➤ keystrokes
keystrokes   keystrokes
{newmacro}   keystrokes
keystrokes ◀───────────────── {RETURN}

LOOPING AND CALLING

The /XG command:

MAIN MACRO	NEW MACRO
keystrokes	keystrokes
keystrokes	keystrokes
/XGnewmacro~	keystrokes
keystrokes	

The {BRANCH} command:

MAIN MACRO	NEW MACRO
keystrokes	keystrokes
keystrokes	keystrokes
{BRANCH newmacro}	keystrokes
keystrokes	

The {DISPATCH} command:

ROUTE cell	MAIN MACRO	NEW MACRO
newmacro	keystrokes	keystrokes
	keystrokes	keystrokes
	{DISPATCH route}	keystrokes
	keystrokes	

{subroutine}

The command {subroutine} tells system to go to another macro cell and continue executing keystrokes. The system returns to the main macro when either a blank cell or a {RETURN} command is encountered in the subroutine. When returning to the main macro, it begins execution with the cell directly beneath the cell containing the {subroutine} command.

The {subroutine} command is used by typing the following into a cell:

{subroutine [arg1],[arg2],...[argn]}

Subroutine is the cell address or range name of the cell containing keystrokes to read.

[arg1],[arg2],... is an optional list of arguments passed to the {DEFINE} command. See page 194 for information on {DEFINE}.

The system assumes that the argument is a label (string) unless the argument is followed by the characters **:V** (:Value). A maximum of 31 arguments and suffix characters can be passed.

NOTE: /XC performs the same function (see below), but does not pass arguments.

NOTE: For an example of command use, see page 190.

/XC (Call)

The /X command tells system to go to another macro cell and continue executing keystrokes. The system returns to the main macro whenever the characters /XR are encountered. When returning to the main macro, it begins execution with the cell directly beneath the cell containing the original /XC command.

The /XC command is used by typing the following into a cell:

/XClocation~

Location is the cell address or range name containing keystrokes to read.

NOTE: {subroutine} performs the same function (see above).

NOTE: For an example of command use, see page 190.

LOOPING AND CALLING

/XR or {RETURN}

The /XR or {RETURNS} command is used in conjunction with the /XC, {subroutine}, or {MENUCALL} command. It tells the system to return to the main (calling) macro. To use the command, type either

/XR~ or {RETURN}.

See page 192 for more information on /XC, page 191 for {subroutine}, and page 200 for {MENUCALL}.

{BRANCH}

The {BRANCH} command tells the system to go to another macro cell and continue executing keystrokes. The {BRANCH} command is used by typing the following into a cell:

{BRANCH location}

Location is the cell address or range name containing keystrokes to branch to.

NOTE: /XG performs the same function (see below).

NOTE: For an example of command use, see page 190.

/XG (GoTo)

The /XG (GOTO) command tells the system to go to another macro cell and continue executing keystrokes. The command is used by typing the following into a cell:

/XGLocation~

Location is the cell address or range name containing keystrokes to read.

NOTE: {BRANCH} performs the same function (see page 193).

NOTE: For an example of command use, see page 190.

{DISPATCH}

{DISPATCH} tells the system to go to another macro cell and continue executing keystrokes. The command is used by typing the following into a cell:

{DISPATCH location}

Location is a single cell that contains the range name of the macro to branch to.

EXAMPLE: The cell named ROUTE is blank. The following macro keystrokes will test for a condition. If the condition is true, the label BRANCH1 will be placed in the ROUTE cell. If the condition is false, the label BRANCH2 will be placed in the ROUTE cell. The {DISPATCH} command will then branch to whichever range is named in the ROUTE cell.

{IF testcell=1}{LET route,"BRANCH1"}
{IF testcell=0}{LET route,"BRANCH2"}
{DISPATCH route}

{DEFINE}

The {DEFINE} command allows you to store arguments which are passed from a main macro to a macro subroutine that is called with the {subroutine} command (see page 191). To use the command, the following must be typed within a cell in the subroutine:

{DEFINE location1,location2,...,locationN}

LOOPING AND CALLING

NOTE: The command must be typed before the cell in the subroutine where the arguments will be used.

location1, location2, ... is the cell address or range name of each argument passed. If the location is preceded with a plus sign (+), the system will assume that the location contains the address of another cell.

The system assumes that the argument is a label (string) unless the location is followed by the characters **:V** (:Value).

NOTE: The {subroutine} and {DEFINE} commands must both have the same number of arguments.

{ONERROR}

The {ONERROR} command will branch a macro if a Lotus error occurs during macro execution. To use this command, the following should be typed into a cell:

{ONERROR branch-location,[message-location]}

branch-location is the cell address or range name containing keystrokes to execute if an error occurs.

message-location is an optional cell address or range name of a cell in which will be stored the error message associated with the error which has occurred.

NOTE: An {ONERROR} command will remain in effect until: an error occurs, another {ONERROR} message is encountered, or the macro ends.

{RESTART}

The {RESTART} command will complete a macro subroutine and then cancel execution of the macro without returning to the main macro. To use the command, type the following into a cell:

{RESTART}

NOTE: For information on calling a subroutine, see page 191.

{FOR}

The {FOR} command will repeat a named **subroutine** for a specified number of loops. To use the command, type the following into a cell:

{FOR counter,start-number,stop-number, step-number,subroutine}

counter is cell address or range name of the cell which will count the number of subroutine repetitions.

start-number is the starting number which will be entered in the counter cell.

stop-number is the number after which subroutine repetitions will end.

step-number is the increment by which the counter will be advanced.

subroutine is the name of the subroutine that will be repeated.

EXAMPLE: {FOR count,1,10,1,print}. This command will place the number 1 in the cell named *count*. This number will increment by one each time the subroutine *print* runs. The subroutine will repeat until the number 10 is reached in the *count* cell. In other words, the subroutine will be repeated ten times.

NOTE: To end a {FOR} loop before the stop-number is reached, use {FORBREAK} (see below).

{FORBREAK}

The {FORBREAK} command will end a {FOR} loop. To use this command, type the following into a cell:

LOOPING AND CALLING 197

{FORBREAK}

Macro execution will proceed with the command directly following the {FOR} command.

EXAMPLE: In the example below, the subroutine *print* will repeat ten times *unless* the test cell equals zero. If that happens, the {FORBREAK} command will route execution back to the main macro as indicated.

MAIN MACRO   PRINT

keystrokes   keystrokes
keystrokes   keystrokes
{FOR count,1,10,1,print}   keystrokes
keystrokes   {IF test=0}{FORBREAK}
keystrokes   keystrokes

NOTE: See above for information on the {FOR} command.

/XI or {IF}

The /XI or {IF} command tells the system that IF a certain condition (a formula that you will input) is TRUE, THEN it should continue executing the keystrokes that appear in the PRESENT macro cell. If the formula in NOT true, the system should execute the keystrokes that appear in the cell BELOW. The command is used by typing one of the following into a cell:

/XIcondition~ or
{IF condition}

EXAMPLE: The macros below test a cell which has the range name *testcell*. If the *testcell* is equal to 10, the system will *quit* macro execution. If not, the system will continue executing the keystrokes that appear below the /XI or {IF} command.

/XItestcell=10~/XQ~   {IF testcell=10}{QUIT}
keystrokes   keystrokes

{SYSTEM}

The {SYSTEM} command executes a specified DOS command. After the DOS command is completed, the system returns to Lotus and resumes macro execution. The {SYSTEM} command is used by typing the following into a cell:

{SYSTEM command}

command is the DOS command to execute.

USER-DEFINED MACRO MENUS

\XM or {MENUBRANCH}

The /XM or {MENUBRANCH} command allows you to construct your own menus. Each menu can have up to eight selections.

The /XM or {MENUBRANCH} command is used by typing one of the following into a cell:

/XMlocation~ or
{MENUBRANCH location}

location is the cell address or range name of the first cell of the menu.

The *menu* consists of the *range name* of the first menu cell, the menu selections, a description for each of these selections, and the commands which are to be executed for each selection.

The example below shows where each of these parts should be typed on the worksheet.

	AA	AB	AC	AD
1	\M	keystrokes		
2		/XMmenuname~		
3				
4	Menuname	Selection1	Selection2	Selection3
5		Description	Description	Descripion
6		Command	Command	Command

	AA	AB	AC	AD
1	\M	keystrokes		
2		{MENUBRANCH menuname}		
3				
4	Menuname	Selection1	Selection2	Selection3
5		Description	Description	Descripion
6		Command	Command	Command

{MENUCALL}

The {MENUCALL} command displays a user-defined menu in the same way as does the {MENUBRANCH} command. When using {MENUCALL}, the system returns to the main macro when either a blank cell or a {RETURN} command is encountered during menu selection command keystroke execution. When returning to the main macro, it begins execution with the cell directly beneath the cell containing the {MENUCALL} command.

To use {MENUCALL}, the following is typed into a cell:

{MENUCALL location}

location is the cell address or range name of the first cell of the menu.

The *menu* consists of the *range name* of the first menu cell, the menu selections, a description for each of these selections, and the commands that are to be executed for each selection.

The example below shows where each of these parts should be typed on the worksheet.

	AA	AB	AC	AD
1	\M	keystrokes		
2		{MENUCALL menuname}		
3				
4	Menuname	Selection1	Selection2	Selection3
5		Description	Description	Descripton
6		Command	Command	Command

Comparison of {MENUBRANCH} and {MENUCALL}

Both the {MENUBRANCH} and {MENUCALL} commands instruct the system to display a user-defined menu and execute keystrokes which correspond to the

USER-DEFINED MACRO MENUS

selection made by the user. However, the {MENUCALL} command tells the system that it will eventually return to main (calling) macro. This will happen whenever the system encounters either a blank cell or the {RETURN} command. When returning to the main macro, it begins execution with the cell directly beneath the cell containing the {MENUCALL} command.

The system *does not* return to main macro when the {MENUBRANCH} command is used.

```
\M          keystrokes
            {MENUCALL menuname}
            keystrokes         ← — — — — — — — — — —
                                                         |
Menuname    Selection1      Selection2      Selection3   |
            Description     Description     Description  |
            Command         Command         Command      |
                |               |               |        |
            — — — — — — — — — — — — — — — — — — — — — —
```

MACRO SUSPENSION

/XQ or {QUIT}

The /XQ or {QUIT} command tells the system to stop the execution of the macro and return control of the system to the user. The command is used by typing one of the following into a cell: **/XQ~** or **{QUIT}**.

{BREAK}

{BREAK} returns the system to the READY mode without interrupting the macro. The command is used by typing the following into a cell: **{BREAK}**.

{WAIT}

The {WAIT} command pauses macro execution for a specified length of time. During the pause, the WAIT indicator is displayed. The command is used by typing the following into a cell:

{WAIT time-number}

time-number is the time at which to end the pause.

EXAMPLE: {WAIT @NOW+@TIME(0,1,0)}. This command line will pause the system for one minute.

USER INPUT

The {?} Command

The {?} command should be typed at the point within macro keystrokes where you want the macro to pause.

During execution, the command will cause the macro to pause. The user can move the cursor, type data, or perform commands during this pause. After the user presses the **ENTER** key, the macro will resume execution at the point directly after the {?} command.

{GET}

The {GET} command will cause the macro to pause and accept input of a single character (number, letter, or key listed on page 166). After the user types the character, the character is stored as a label in a cell location specified in the command. The macro will resume execution at the point directly after the command.

The command is used by typing the following into a cell:

{GET location}

location is a cell address or range name of a cell in which the input string will be stored.

/XL or {GETLABEL}

The /XL or {GETLABELS} command will cause the macro to pause, display a message that you have specified, and accept input of a character string (label).

After the user types the string and presses the **ENTER** key, the string will appear either in the present cursor cell or in a cell location specified in the command. The macro will resume execution at the point directly after the command.

The command is used by typing one of the following into a cell:

/XLprompt~location~ or
{GETLABEL prompt,location}

prompt is the message that will be displayed during the pause.

location is an optional cell address or range name of a cell in which the input string will be stored. If no location is specified, the input string will appear at the current pointer location.

/XN or {GETNUMBER}

The /XN or {GETNUMBERS} command will cause the macro to pause, display a message that you have specified, and accept input of a character value (number) or a formula. After the user types the value and presses the ENTER key, the value will appear either in the present cursor cell or in a cell location specified in the command. The macro will resume execution at the point directly after the command.

The command is used by typing one of the following into a cell:

/XNprompt~location~ or
{GETNUMBER prompt,location}

USER INPUT

prompt is the message that will be displayed during the pause.

location is an optional cell address or range name of a cell in which the input value will be stored. If no location is specified, the input value will appear at the current pointer location.

{LOOK}

The {LOOK} command will cause the macro to check the keyboard buffer for a single character (number, letter, or key listed on page 66). If it finds a character, the character will be stored as a label in a cell location specified in the command. If it finds several characters, the first character found will be stored. If no character appears in the buffer, an apostrophe (label prefix) will be stored in the cell location specified. The macro will continue execution at the point directly after the command.

The command is used by typing the following into a cell:

{LOOK location}

location is a cell address or range name of a cell in which the character will be stored.

SPREADSHEET MANIPULATION

{BLANK}

The {BLANK} command erases the contents of a cell or range of cells. The command is used by typing the following into a cell:

{BLANK location}

location is a cell address, range of cells or range name of cells to blank.

{CONTENTS}

The {CONTENTS} command copies the contents of a cell into another cell. The copy will appear as a label. {CONTENTS} is used to copy values or formulas as a string that can then be manipulated with string functions (see pages 35–38). The command is used by typing the following into a cell:

{CONTENTS target-location,source-location, [width],[cell-format]}

target-location is a cell address or range name of a cell in which the label will appear.

source-location is the cell address or range name of the material to be copied.

width is the optional width of the copied material (maximum 240 characters).

cell-format is the optional code number that represents a cell format in which the copied material will appear. The following codes can be used:

0 to 15	Fixed, 0-15 decimals
16 to 31	Scientific, 0-15 decimals

SPREADSHEET MANIPULATION

32 to 47	Currency, 0-15 decimals
48 to 63	Percent, 0-15 decimals
64 to 79	Comma, 0-15 decimals
112	+/-
113	General
114	D1 (DD-MMM-YY)
115	D2 (DD-MMM)
116	D3 (MMM-YY)
117	Text
118	Hidden
119	D6 (HH:MM:SS AM/PM)
120	D7 (HH:MM AM/PM)
121	D4 (Long Intn'l Date)
122	D5 (Short Intn'l Date)
123	D8 (Long Intn'l Time)
124	D9 (Short Intn'l Time)
127	Worksheet's global cell format

{LET}

The {LET} command will enter a specified value or label into a specified cell. The command is used by typing the following into a cell:

{LET location,entry}

location is a cell address or range name of a cell in which the entry will appear.

entry is the entry to appear in the cell. This entry can be a value, string, formula, or the cell address of another cell. If the entry is a formula, the system evaluates the formula and enters the result of that formula in the location. If the entry is a value, it will appear as a value in the location unless it is followed by the characters **:L** (:Label). If the entry is a character string, it will appear as a label in the location unless it is followed by the characters **:V** (:Value).

{PUT}

The {PUT} command will enter a specified value or label into a specified cell within a range of cells. The command is used by typing the following into a cell:

{LET location,column-offset,row-offset,entry}

location is the range address or range name containing the cell in which the entry will appear.

column-offset is the column position of the target cell within the specified range. The first column of the range has an offset of 0, the second column has an offset of 1, and so on.

row-offset is the row position of the target cell within the specified range. The first row of the range has an offset of 0, the second row has an offset of 1, and so on.

entry is the entry to appear in the cell. This entry can be a value, string, formula or the cell address of another cell. If the entry is a formula, the system evaluates the formula and enters the result of that formula in the location. If the entry is a value, it will appear as a value in the location unless it is followed by the characters **:L** (:Label). If the entry is a character string, it will appear as a label in the location unless it is followed by the characters **:V** (:Value).

{RECALC}

The {RECALC} command recalculates (by row) a specified range of cells. (To recalculate by column, see below.) The command is used by typing the following into a cell:

{RECALC location,[condition],[iterations]}

location is the cell address, range address or range name of the cells to recalculate.

condition is an optional formula that will be evaluated by the system. Recalculation will repeat until this formula evaluates as true.

iterations is an optional number of times to repeat recalculation. Iteration cannot be specified unless a condition is present.

{RECALCCOL}

The {RECALCCOL} command recalculates (by column) a specified range of cells. (To recalculate by row, see above.) The command is used by typing the following into a cell:

{RECALCCOL location,[condition],[iterations]}

location is the cell address, range address or range name of the cells to recalculate.

condition is an optional formula which will be evaluated by the system. Recalculation will repeat until this formula evaluates as true.

iterations is an optional number of times to repeat recalculation. Iteration cannot be specified unless a condition is present.

CONTROLLING ENVIRONMENT

{BEEP}

The {BEEP} command will sound a specified computer tone. The command is used by typing the following into a cell:

{BEEP [tone-number]}

tone-number is a number from 1 to 4 that signifies which of your computer's tones will be sounded.

{BORDERSOFF}/{BORDERSON} or {FRAMEOFF}/{FRAMEON}

The {BORDERSOFF} and {FRAMEOFF} commands will suppress the display of the spreadsheet border column letters and row numbers. The {BORDERSON} and {FRAMEON} commands will redisplay these letters and numbers.

{BREAKOFF}/{BREAKON}

Pressing **CTRL+BREAK** from the keyboard will normally halt macro execution. The {BREAKOFF} command will disable **CTRL+BREAK**. The {BREAKON} command will again enable the ability of **CTRL+BREAK** to halt a macro.

{GRAPHOFF}/{GRAPHON}

The {GRAPHON} command will either make a named graph current and/or display the graph, depending on which of the optional arguments are used. The command is used by typing the following into a cell:

{GRAPHON [named-graph],[nodisplay]}.

Typing {GRAPHON} with no arguments will display the *current graph*.

named-graph is the optional name of a graph to make current. Typing {GRAPHON named-graph} will make a new graph current and display that graph.

nodisplay suppresses display of a named graph. Typing {GRAPHON named-graph,nodisplay} will make a new graph current but will not display that graph.

The {GRAPHOFF} command will clear any graph from the screen.

{INDICATE}

The {INDICATE} command will display a specified mode indicator. The command is used by typing the following into a cell:

{INDICATE [string]}

string is the character string that will appear as the mode indicator.

NOTE: Typing {INDICATE} without specifying a character string will return the mode indicator to its default (see list on page 13).

{PANELOFF}/{PANELON}

The {PANELOFF} command will suppress changes in the display of the control panel and status line that normally occur when commands are executed by a macro. The command is used by typing the following into a cell:

{PANELOFF [clear]}

clear is this option will clear the control panel and status line before turning the panel off.

The {PANELON} command will return the control panel and status line to normal.

{WINDOWSOFF}/{WINDOWSON}

The {WINDOWSOFF} command will suppress changes in the display of the worksheet and borders that normally occur when commands are executed by a macro.

The {WINDOWSON} command will return the control worksheet and border display to normal.

TEXT FILE MANIPULATION

{OPEN}

The {OPEN} command opens a new or existing text file. The command is used by typing the following into a cell:

{OPEN file-name,access-type}.

file-name is the name of the text file to open.

access-type is the type of access that will be allowed in the open text file. The selections are:

r Characters can be *read* from an existing file. The pointer will be placed at the beginning of the file. {READ}, {READLN}, {GETPOS}, or {SETPOS} can be used on this type of file.

w Characters can be stored in (*written to*) a new file; or stored in or read from an existing file. The pointer will be placed at the beginning of the file; therefore, if characters are written to an existing file, they will overwrite any characters already in the file. {READ}, {READLN}, {WRITE}, {WRITELN}, {GETPOS}, or {SETPOS} can be used on this type of file.

m Characters can be stored in or read from an existing file. The pointer will be placed at the beginning of the file, therefore if characters are written to the file, they will overwrite any characters already in the file. {READ}, {READLN}, {WRITE}, {WRITELN}, {GETPOS}, or {SETPOS} can be used on this type of file.

a Characters can be stored in or read from an existing file. The pointer will be placed at the *end* of the file, therefore if characters are written to the file, they be *appended to* any characters already in the file. {READ}, {READLN}, {WRITE}, {WRITELN}, {GETPOS}, or {SETPOS} can be used on this type of file.

{CLOSE}

The {CLOSE} command closes the open text file. The command is used by typing the following into a cell:

{CLOSE}

NOTE: The system will not read or execute any macro commands that appear in a cell after the {CLOSE} command. It *will* continue executing commands in the cell *below* the {CLOSE} command.

{READ}

The {READ} command will read a specified number of characters from the open text file and place those characters in a cell on the spreadsheet. The command is used by typing the following into a cell:

{READ byte-count,location}

byte-count is the number of bytes (characters) to read.

NOTE: Reading begins at the current pointer location within the text file. For information on moving the pointer, see page 216.

location is the cell address or range name of the cell in which characters will be stored on the spreadsheet.

NOTE: See page 213 for information on opening a text file.

{READLN}

The {READLN} command will read a line of characters from the open text file and place those characters in a cell on the spreadsheet. The command is used by typing the following into a cell:

{READLN location}

NOTE: Reading begins at the current pointer location within the text file. For information on moving the pointer, see page 216.

location is the cell address or range name of the cell in which characters will be stored on the spreadsheet.

NOTE: See page 213 for information on opening a text file.

{WRITE}

The {WRITE} command will write specified characters to the open text file. The command is used by typing the following into a cell:

{WRITE string}

string is the characters that will be stored in the text file.

NOTE: Writing begins at the current pointer location within the text file. For information on moving the pointer, see page 216.

NOTE: See page 213 for information on opening a text file.

{WRITELN}

The {WRITELN} command will write specified characters, a carriage return, and a line feed to the open text file. The command is used by typing the following into a cell:

{WRITELN string}

string is the characters that will be stored in the text file.

NOTE: Writing begins at the current pointer location within the text file. For information on moving the pointer, see page 216.

NOTE: See page 213 for information on opening a text file.

{FILESIZE}

The {FILESIZE} command will count the number of bytes in the open text file and store that number in a cell on the spreadsheet. The command is used by typing the following into a cell:

{FILESIZE location}

location is the cell address or range name of the cell in which the file size will be stored on the spreadsheet.

NOTE: See page 213 for information on opening a text file.

{GETPOS}

The {GETPOS} command will determine the pointer position in the open text file and store that number in a cell on the spreadsheet. The command is used by typing the following into a cell:

{GETPOS location}

location is the cell address or range name of the cell in which the pointer position will be stored on the spreadsheet.

NOTE: To move the pointer, see the {SETPOS} command below.

NOTE: See page 213 for information on opening a text file.

{SETPOS}

The {SETPOS} command will move the pointer in the open text file. The command is used by typing the following into a cell:

{SETPOS offset-number}

offset-number is the byte at which to position the pointer. The first byte of the file is 0, the second is 1, and so on.

NOTE: To determine the current pointer position, see the {GETPOS} command above.

NOTE: See page 213 for information on opening a text file.

Different Macros can Perform the Same Task

Macros containing different keystrokes can accomplish the same tasks. For example:

this macro	and	this macro
{GOTO}B3~		{HOME}{DOWN}{DOWN}{RIGHT}
JAN{RIGHT}		JAN~{RIGHT}

will input the same label in the same location on the worksheet.

Debugging Problem Macros

Mistakes (or "bugs") in macros will be easier to find if the following tips are used:

- It is important to perform the desired operation and write down keystrokes before typing them into a macro. One or more keystrokes are often forgotten when memory is relied upon.

- Write and test macros in small pieces.

- Use step execution (**ALT+F2**—see page 106) to watch each step of macro. Errors are easier to spot if macro is executing one step at a time.

- Many times a macro does not work properly because one or more tildes (~) which represent the ENTER keystroke are missing.

SAMPLE DATABASE

A PORTION OF A SAMPLE DATABASE

	A	B	C	D	E
1	Employee Database				
2					
3	LNAME	FNAME	DIVISION	HIRE DATE	SALARY
4	Fuller	Walter	Service	15-Jan-81	19,000
5	Chapin	Mark	Accounting	01-Apr-81	20,000
6	Adams	Anne	Administration	21-Jul-81	15,000
7	Frantzen	Jason	Sales	02-Sep-81	32,500
8	Baker	Joan	Sales	15-Apr-82	45,000
9	Schonberger	Peter	Sales	06-Jun-82	25,000
10	Ruttenberg	Ruth	Administration	18-Aug-82	27,000
11	Smythe	Nancy	Sales	02-Nov-82	42,000
12	Bushman	Stanley	Sales	15-Jan-83	45,000
13	Bazdaz	Raphael	Service	05-Feb-83	35,000
14	Clements	William	Service	14-Feb-83	21,000
15	Sylvester	Ron	Accounting	14-Mar-83	30,000
16	Feldman	Bob	Service	01-Apr-83	19,500
17	Dixon	Gary	Administration	07-Jun-83	17,000
18	Schulte	Dale	Accounting	15-Jun-83	25,000
19					

	LNAME	FNAME	DIVISION	HIRE DATE	SALARY
20					
21	LNAME				
22	S*				
23					
24					
25	LNAME	FNAME	DIVISION	HIRE DATE	SALARY
26	Schulte	Dale	Accounting	15-Jun-83	25,000
27	Sylvester	Ron	Accounting	14-Mar-83	30,000
28	Smythe	Nancy	Sales	02-Nov-82	42,000

RECORD - Each of the rows 4 through 18.
FIELD - Each cell within these rows.
FIELD NAME - The contents of each cell in row 3.
DATABASE - The collection of all records, fields and field names.

DATA RANGE - range of data to be sorted - does not include the row containing the field names (A4..E18)

INPUT RANGE - Database itself - including field names (A3..E18)

CRITERIA RANGE HEADINGS - Headings in row 21
SPECIFIC CRITERION - Input in cell A22
CRITERIA RANGE - Range containing specific criteria, including criteria field names (A21..E22)

OUTPUT RANGE HEADINGS - Headings in row 25
OUTPUT RANGE - range containing output field names and the area in which the extracted list will appear (A25..E28)

DATABASE GENERAL INFORMATION

Database Terminology

RECORD All related bits of information are called RECORDS. In Lotus, each row of information on the screen is a RECORD.

NOTE: In the sample database that appears on page 218, each row represents one RECORD. For example, all of the information in row 8 (relating to Joan Baker) is one RECORD:

Baker   Joan   Sales   15-Apr-82   45,000

FIELD Each bit of information within a record is called a FIELD. In the record that appears above, the last name, Baker, occupies one field. So does the first name (Joan), the division (Sales), the hire date (15-Apr-82), and the salary (45,000). Each field occupies a separate cell in Lotus database.

FIELD NAME Each FIELD is assigned a unique FIELD NAME. The FIELD NAMES for the sample database on page 218 appear in row 3.

DATABASE The collection of all records, fields and field names (entire file) is called the DATABASE.

Setting up the Database

To create a new database, you must start with a blank worksheet grid (if necessary, use the /WE command to clear the screen). When typing the new database:

1. Type FIELD NAMES in one row of the worksheet. Each FIELD NAME should be unique and somewhat descriptive of the field that it represents.

DATABASE GENERAL INFORMATION

The row containing the FIELD NAMES should be near the top of the worksheet. All RECORDS will be input BELOW the row containing the FIELD NAMES.

2. Type the desired database RECORDS.

   Each RECORD occupies one row on the worksheet. Each FIELD occupies one cell within that row.

   The information input in each FIELD can be either a label or a value.

   The first RECORD must appear on the line directly below the row containing the FIELD NAMES.

3. Use the **/F**ile **S**ave command to save the database file.

The Data Command

All database manipulation in 1-2-3 is done via the DATA command. To begin the Data command:

1. Press the SLASH (/) key.

   The Main Menu will appear.

2. Type **D** to select **D**ata.

   The Data Menu will appear.

Data Menu Selections

Below is a list of selections from the Data Menu:

Fill Fill a range with a sequence of values (see page 238).

Table Construct a table of values (see page 239).

Sort Sort the records on up to two key field attributes. A sort may be done in ascending or descending order (see pages 233–235).

Query Extract, find, or delete records that meet specified criteria (see pages 223–232).

Distribution Determine the frequency distribution of a range (see page 239).

Matrix Manipulates data stored within a matrix of contiguous rows and columns. This matrix can be inverted (see page 244) or multiplied (see page 244).

Regression This selection allows regression analysis (see page 245).

Parse Transforms a column of labels into a range of labels, values, dates, and times (see page 247).

DATA QUERIES

Find Records — /DQF

The FIND command will tell the system to find all records containing a specified criterion.

1. Set the Criteria for the search:

    a. Copy the database Field Names to another part of the worksheet. These copied field names become the *Criteria Range Headings*.

    b. Type the desired Criteria under the appropriate headings.

    For more information about specifying criteria, see page 230.

    NOTE: Criteria Range Headings and specific Criteria must be typed EXACTLY as they appear in the database that you are searching. For example, if the database Field Names are in all capital letters, the Criteria Range Headings must be in all capital letters. In the same way, if the information input in the field appears in uppercase and lowercase (initial caps) the Specific Criteria must be in uppercase and lowercase.

2. Begin the Data Query command:

    a. Press the SLASH (/) key.

    b. Type **D** to select **D**ata.

    c. Type **Q** to select **Q**uery.

    The Query Menu and Query Setting Screen will appear. The Setting Screen contains the current settings for input range, criteria range, and output range.

3. Specify the Input Range:

    a. Type **I** to select **I**nput.

    The prompt "Enter input range" will appear. The Input Range consists of the database itself and its field names.

    b. Point to (or type) the range containing the database and field names.

    See page 218 for an example of an Input Range.

    c. Press **ENTER** to accept the range.

4. Specify the Criteria Range:

    a. Type **C** to select **C**riteria.

    The prompt "Enter criteria range" will appear. The criteria range consists of the cells containing the specified criteria and the criteria range headings.

    b. Point to (or type) the range containing the criteria and the criteria range heading(s).

    See page 218 for an example of Criteria Range.

    c. Press **ENTER** to accept the range.

5. Type **F** to **F**ind records.

    The first record satisfying the criteria will appear highlighted on the screen. Each time the **DOWN ARROW** is pressed, the *next record* will be found and highlighted. Each time the **UP ARROW** is pressed, the *previous record* will be found and highlighted.

    NOTE: The system will beep when trying to move past the first or last record in the database.

6. Press **ESC** (or **ENTER**) to end the Find procedure. The Query Menu and Query Setting Screen will reappear.

    NOTE: Input and Criteria ranges remain in the system's memory until they are respecified or RESET (see **/D**ata **Q**uery **R**eset, page 229). As long as these ranges are in memory, the most recent Find can be repeated from the READY mode by using the **F7** (QUERY) key (see page 230).

Extract Records — /DQE

The EXTRACT command will compile a separate listing of all records that match a specified criteria.

1. Set the Criteria for the extract:

    a. Copy the database Field Names to another part of the worksheet. These copied field names become the *Criteria Range Headings*.

    b. Type the desired *Criteria* under the appropriate headings.

    For more information about specifying criteria, see page 230.

    NOTE: Criteria Range Headings and specific Criteria must be typed EXACTLY as they appear in the database that you are searching. For example, if the database Field Names are in all capital letters, the Criteria Range Headings must be in all capital letters. In the same way, if the information input in the field appears in uppercase and lowercase (initial caps) the Specific Criteria must be in uppercase and lowercase.

2. Set the Output Range Headings:

    - Copy the database Field Names to another part of the worksheet. These copied field names become the *Output Range Headings*.

    NOTE: Output Range Headings (like Criteria Range Headings) must be typed EXACTLY as they appear in the database that you are extracting from.

3. Begin the Data Query command:

   a. Press the SLASH (/) key.

   b. Type **D** to select **D**ata.

   c. Type **Q** to select **Q**uery.

   The Query Menu and Query Setting Screen will appear. The Setting Screen contains the current settings for input range, criteria range, and output range.

4. Specify the Input Range:

   a. Type **I** to select **I**nput.

   The prompt "Enter input range" will appear. The Input Range consists of the data base records to sort and their field names.

   b. Point to (or type) the range containing the database and field names.

   See page 218 for an example of an Input Range.

   c. Press **ENTER** to accept the range.

5. Specify the Criteria Range:

   a. Type **C** to select **C**riteria.

   The prompt "Enter criteria range" will appear. The criteria range consists of the cells containing the specified criteria and the criteria range headings.

   b. Point to (or type) the range containing the criteria and the criteria range heading(s).

   See page 218 for an example of Criteria Range.

   c. Press **ENTER** to accept the range.

6. Specify the Output Range:

   a. Type **O** to select **O**utput.

   The prompt "Enter output range" will appear. The output range consists of the cells containing the Output Field Names and the area in which the extracted records will appear.

b. Point to (or type) the range containing the output field names and the blank rows that will hold extracted records.

See page xx for an example of Output Range.

c. Press **ENTER** to accept the range.

NOTE: A sufficient amount of space to hold extracted records must be specified in the range. If an insufficient amount of space is specified in the range, the message "Too many records for output range" will appear during the extract.

7. Type **E** to **E**xtract records.

Copies of records meeting the criteria will appear in the Output Range.

NOTE: Input, Criterion and Output ranges remain in the system's memory until they are respecified or RESET (see **/D**ata **Q**uery **R**eset, page 229). As long as these ranges are in memory, the most recent Extract can be repeated from the READY mode by using the **F7** (QUERY) key (see page 230).

Extract Unique Records — /DQU

The UNIQUE command will eliminate duplicate records from being copied to the output range during a Data Extract. To use this command:

1. Follow Steps 1 through 6 on page 225 (**/D**ata **E**xtract command).

2. Type **U** to select **U**nique.

Copies of records meeting the criteria will appear in the Output Range. Duplicate records will be ignored.

Delete Records — /DQD

The DELETE command will delete all records that match a specified criteria.

1. Set the Criteria for the deletion:

   a. Copy the database Field Names to another part of the worksheet. These copied field names become the *Criteria Range Headings*.

   b. Type the desired *Criteria* under the appropriate headings.

   For more information about specifying criteria, see page 230.

   NOTE: Criteria Range Headings and specific Criteria must be typed EXACTLY as they appear in the database that you are searching. For example, if the database Field Names are in all capital letters, the Criteria Range Headings must be in all capital letters. In the same way, if the information input in the field appears in uppercase and lowercase (initial caps) the Specific Criteria must be in uppercase and lowercase.

2. Begin the Data Query command:

   a. Press the SLASH (/) key.

   b. Type **D** to select **D**ata.

   c. Type **Q** to select **Q**uery.

   The Query Menu and Query Setting Screen will appear. The Setting Screen contains the current settings for input range, criteria range, and output range.

3. Specify the Input Range:

   a. Type **I** to select **I**nput.

   The prompt "Enter input range" will appear. The Input Range consists of the database itself and its field names.

b. Point to (or type) the range containing the data base and field names.

See page 218 for an example of an Input Range.

c. Press **ENTER** to accept the range.

4. Specify the Criteria Range:

a. Type **C** to select **C**riteria.

The prompt "Enter criteria range" will appear. The criteria range consists of the cells containing the specified criteria and the criteria range headings.

b. Point to (or type) the range containing the criteria and the criteria range heading(s).

See page 218 for an example of Criteria Range.

c. Press **ENTER** to accept the range.

5. Type **D** to **D**elete records.

A verification menu will appear.

6. Confirm or abort the deletion:

- Type **C** to **C**ancel the deletion, or
- Type **D** to select **D**elete.

The Data Query Menu will reappear. Any blank rows caused by the deletion will be automatically filled in by the system.

NOTE: Input and Criteria ranges remain in the system's memory until they are respecified or RESET (see **/D**ata **Q**uery **R**eset, below). As long as these ranges are in memory, the most recent Find can be repeated from the READY mode by using the **F7** (QUERY) key (see page 230).

Data Query Reset — /DQR

Input, Criterion, and Output ranges remain in the system's memory until they are respecified or RESET. To reset these ranges:

1. Press the SLASH (/) key.

   The Main Menu will appear.

2. Type **D** to select **D**ata.

   The Data Menu will appear.

3. Type **Q** to select **Q**uery.

   The Query Menu and Query Setting screen will appear.

4. Type **R** to select **R**eset.

   All ranges will be cleared.

   NOTE: These ranges must then be respecified prior to Extracting, Finding, or Deleting any additional records.

Data Query Quit — /DQQ

This Quit selection will Quit the query menu and return you to the Data Menu.

F7 (QUERY) Key

The **F7** (QUERY) key will repeat the most recent set of data specifications (the most recently specified Input, Criteria, and Output ranges and most recently specified query function: Find, Extract, or Delete).

The **F7** key is used from the READY mode.

Specifying Criteria

The criteria is typed in the cell directly below the Criteria Range Heading to which the criteria relates. For example, if you want to find employees with a specific LASTNAME, the criteria should be typed below the Criteria Range Heading LASTNAME. See the diagram on page 218 for an example of properly placed criteria.

If you want to specify criteria for multiple fields, each

criteria statement should appear below the appropriate Criteria Range Heading. If you want the search to satisfy the condition of *both* (or all) criteria specified, place both (or all) criteria on the same row within the criteria range. If you want the search to satisfy the condition of *either* criteria, type both (or all) criteria on different rows within the range.

Different types of criteria may be specified:

> **Exact Match** By typing a character string or a value as criteria, the system will find (or extract, or delete) only those records containing an exact match for that character string or value.
>
> **Wildcards** When typing the criteria, WILDCARDS can be used. A WILDCARD is a character (either a question mark or an asterisk) that can be used to represent one or more characters within the criteria.

NOTE: An asterisk (*) can represent any number of characters. For example, if you specify the system extract all records with the LAST NAME of B*, it will find all records with LAST NAMES that begin with the letter "B," no matter how many letters are in the name. If you specify a LAST NAME of BA* it will find all records with LAST NAMES that begin with the letters "BA," again, no matter how many letters are in the name. If you specify B*Z, all names beginning with "B" and ending with "Z." Any amount of letters may appear between these two letters.

NOTE: A question mark (?) represents only one character. If you specify a criterion of B? the system will find ONLY two letter names whose first letter is "B." If you specify B??, the system will find only THREE letter names whose first letter is "B." Each question mark represents one character.

> **Exclusion** A tilde (~) can be used in the criteria to exclude a specific character string. If you specify ~Administration as the criteria under the field name DIVISION, the system will find all records except those with Administration as the division.

Criteria that Incorporate Comparisons It is possible to specify criteria that incorporate comparisons. For example, you can Find all records of those employees with Salaries GREATER THAN $25,000. Or with Employee ID Numbers LESS THAN OR EQUAL TO 25. This is done by simply using standard operators when inputting the criteria:

>	greater than
<	less than
=	equals

NOTE: For a complete list of operators, see page 24.

For example, to EXTRACT all records of those employees whose SALARY is GREATER THAN $30,000, the criterion to input would be constructed as follows:

SALARY   is GREATER THAN $30000

+E4   >   30000

NOTE: E4 is the first cell containing a SALARY in the database.

SORTING RECORDS

General Information

The DATA SORT command allows you to rearrange the records in a database, either in alphabetical or numerical order.

1. Begin the Data Sort command:

    a. Press the SLASH (/) key.

    b. Type **D** to select **D**ata.

    c. Type **S** to select **S**ort.

    The Sort Menu and Sort Setting Screen will appear. The Setting Screen contains the current settings for data range, primary key field, primary key sort order, secondary key field, and secondary key sort order.

2. Specify the Data Range:

    a. Type **D** to select **D**ata-Range.

    The prompt "Enter data range" will appear. The Data Range consists of the data base itself *without* its field names.

    b. Point to (or type) the range containing the database.

    See page 218 for an example of a Data Range.

    c. Press **ENTER** to accept the range.

3. Specify the Primary Key (the primary column by which to sort the database) and Primary Key Sort Order:

    a. Type **P** to select **P**rimary-key.

    The prompt "Primary sort key" will appear.

    b. Point to (or type) any coordinate within the column containing the field to be sorted.

c. Press **ENTER** to accept the range.

The prompt "Sort order (A or D)" will appear.

d. Specify the sort order:

- Type **A** to sort the records in **A**scending order (A to Z or numerically ascending), or
- Type **D** to sort the database in **D**escending order (Z to A or numerically descending).

e. Press **ENTER**.

4. If desired, specify a Secondary key (the secondary column by which to sort the database) and Secondary Key Sort Order:

   a. Type **S** to select **S**econdary-key.

   The prompt "Secondary sort key" will appear.

   b. Point to (or type) any coordinate within the column containing the field to be sorted.

   c. Press **ENTER** to accept the range.

   The prompt "Sort order (A or D)" will appear.

   d. Specify the sort order:

   - Type **A** to sort the records in **A**scending order (A to Z or numerically ascending), or
   - Type **D** to sort the database in **D**escending order (Z to A or numerically descending).

   e. Press **ENTER**.

5. Type **G** to select **G**o and begin the sort.
   The system will sort the records and return to the READY mode.

   NOTE: Data range, primary sort key, secondary sort key, and sort order (ascending or descending) remain in the system's memory until they are respecified or RESET (see **/D**ata **S**ort Reset, page 229). As long as these specifications are in memory, the most recent Sort can be repeated from the READY mode by using the **F7** (QUERY) key (see page 230).

Data Sort Reset — /DSR

Data range, primary sort key, secondary sort key, and sort order (ascending or descending) remain in the system's memory until they are respecified or RESET. To reset these ranges:

1. Press the SLASH (/) key.

    The Main Menu will appear.

2. Type **D** to select **D**ata.

    The Data Menu will appear.

3. Type **S** to select **S**ort.

    The Sort Menu will appear.

4. Type **R** to select **R**eset.

    All ranges will be cleared.

    NOTE: These settings must be respecified prior to Sorting any additional records.

DATABASE STATISTICAL FUNCTIONS

The Database Statistical Functions are used to summarize database information. Following is a listing of these functions:

@DAVG Calculate AVERAGE values in a specified field in only those database records that meet a given criteria.

@DCOUNT COUNT elements in a specified field in only those database records that meet a given criteria.

@DMAX Find the MAXIMUM value in a specified field in only those database records that meet a given criteria.

@DMIN Find the MINIMUM value in a specified field in only those database records that meet a given criteria.

@DSTD Find the STANDARD deviation in a specified field in only those database records that meet a given criteria.

@DSUM Calculate the SUM of values in a specified field in only those database records that meet a given criteria.

@DVAR Find the VARIANCE of values in a specified field in only those database records that meet a given criteria.

All of these functions are used by typing the following into a cell:

@FUNCTION(Input range,Field Offset,Criteria range)

1. The first character typed must be the symbol **@**.
2. Type the **Function** name.

   EXAMPLE: **DAVG**.

3. Type the **input range**, **field offset**, and **criterion range** (separated by commas) within parentheses.

Input range is the range address or range name of the database.

Field offset is the field (column) in the database to use in the calculation. To determine the offset, count the columns in the input range starting with zero for the first column.

Criteria range is the cells containing the specified criteria and the criteria range headings. For more information on specifying criteria, see page 230.

EXAMPLE: In the sample database on page 218, the following formula would average the salaries of all employees whose last names begin with S:

@DAVG(A3..E18,4,21..E22)

MISCELLANEOUS DATA COMMANDS

Data Fill — /DF

The Data Fill command will fill a range of cells with a series of numbers. To use the DATA FILL command:

1. Press the SLASH (/) key.

   The Main Menu will appear.

2. Type **D** to select **D**ata.

   The Data Menu will appear.

3. Type **F** to select **F**ill.

   The prompt "Enter Fill range" will appear.

4. Point to (or type) the range of cells that you wish to fill with numbers and press **ENTER**.

   The prompt "Start" will appear. The system is asking for the first (starting) number with which to fill the range.

5. Type the FIRST NUMBER that will appear in the range and press **ENTER**.

   The prompt "Step" will appear. The system is asking for the interval (step) that will be used between numbers.

6. Type the number that represents the INTERVAL and press **ENTER**.

   NOTE: The number representing the interval may be the decimal equivalent of any fraction (Example: .5 or .75) and/or a negative number.

   The prompt "Stop" will appear. The system is asking for the last (stop) number to fill the range.

7. Type the LAST NUMBER that will appear in the range and press **ENTER**.

   The range of numbers will appear in the designated range of cells.

MISCELLANEOUS DATA COMMANDS   239

Frequency Distribution — /DD

The Distribution subcommand may be used to summarize a set of values within a database or to do quick analyses of raw data. Used in conjunction with 1-2-3's built-in statistical functions, the Distribution subcommand can form the foundation of a user-developed statistical analysis system.

1. Press the SLASH (/) key.

   The Main Menu will appear.

2. Type **D** to select **D**ata.

   The Data Menu will appear.

3. Type **D** to select **D**istribution.

   The prompt "Enter values range" will appear. The "values range" is the range containing the set of numbers to be summarized and/or analyzed.

4. Point to (or type) the range containing values.

5. Press **ENTER** to accept the range.

   The prompt "Enter bin range" will appear.

6. Point to (or type) the bin range.

   NOTE: Bin range values should be in ascending order down a column.

   NOTE: There must be a blank column next to the bin range.

7. Press **ENTER** to accept the range.

   The system will determine how many values in the Value range are less than or equal to each number in the Bin range and will record the results in the column immediately to the right of the Bin range.

Create Data Table — /DT

A DATA TABLE will allow you to "test" the results of certain value changes on specified worksheet cells.

A DATA TABLE has three parts:

- A column or row containing the AMOUNTS TO BE TESTED.
- The FORMULA on which the amounts will be tested.
- Space available for the RESULTS OF THE TESTED AMOUNTS.

   NOTE: Refer to the SAMPLE DATA TABLE on page 242 for examples of Data Table construction.

After the Data Table is constructed, the DATA TABLE COMMAND is used to instruct the system to fill in the outcome of the tests.

To construct a Data Table and use the DATA TABLE COMMAND:

1. Type the column or row of amounts to be tested.

   NOTE: The DATA FILL command can be used to do this (see page 238).

2. Type the formula on which amounts will be tested.

   NOTE: Refer to the SAMPLE DATA TABLE on page 242 for examples of Data Table construction.

3. Press the SLASH (/) key.

   The Main Menu will appear.

4. Type **D** to select **D**ata.

   The Data Menu will appear.

5. Type **T** to select **T**able.

   The Data Table Menu will appear. The selection "1" should be used when you are working with "One input cell, one or more dependent formulas." The selection "2" should be used when you are working with "Two input cells, one dependent formula."

   NOTE: An "INPUT CELL" is the cell through which the values are tested.

MISCELLANEOUS DATA COMMANDS   241

6. Type either **1** or **2**.

   The Prompt "Enter Table range" will appear. The table range is the range of cells that contain the list of amounts to be tested, the formula on which these amounts will be tested, and the space in which the results of the tested amounts will appear.

7. Point to (or type) the table range and press **ENTER**.

   The prompt "Enter Input cell 1" will appear. The input cell is the cell through which we are testing the values.

8. Point to (or type) the coordinate of the first input cell and press **ENTER**.

   If you selected "2" (Two input cells, one dependent formula) in Step 6 above, the prompt "Enter Input cell 2" will appear.

9. If necessary, point to (or type) the coordinate of the second input cell and press **ENTER**.

   The system will fill the Data Table with calculated values and return to the READY mode.

Repeat Data Table — F8

The **F8** key can be used to repeat the most recent Data Table operation (see above).

Data Table Reset — /DTR

To reset all Data Table settings:

1. Press the SLASH (/) key.
   The Main Menu will appear.

2. Type **D** to select **D**ata.
   The Data Menu will appear.

3. Type **T** to select **T**able.
   The Data Table Menu will appear.

4. Type **R** to select **R**eset.
   The system will return to the READY mode.

EXAMPLE - SPREADSHEET CONTAINING A COMPLETED DATA TABLE

	A	B	C	D	E
1	Price/Unit	$4.50			
2	Cost/Unit	$2.80			
3	Unit Sales	100,000	150,000	150,000	200,000
4		1ST Q	2ND Q	3RD Q	4TH Q
5					
6	Sales	$450,000	$675,000	$675,000	$900,000
7	Cost of Goods	280,000	420,000	420,000	560,000
8		--------	--------	--------	--------
9	Gross Profit	170,000	255,000	255,000	340,000
10	Fixed Costs	300,000	300,000	300,000	300,000
11		--------	--------	--------	--------
12	Net Profit	(130,000)	(45,000)	(45,000)	40,000
13					

MISCELLANEOUS DATA COMMANDS

```
14   Total Profit  @SUM(B12..E12)
15       $4.50       (180,000)
16       $4.60       (120,000)
17       $4.70        (60,000)
18       $4.80              0
19       $4.90         60,000
20       $5.00        120,000
```

THE PARTS OF THE TABLE

```
                  ----------------------------------
                  : Total Profit  @SUM(B12..E12) :         FORMULA
                  :------------------------------:         ON WHICH
                  :     $4.50       (180,000)    :         AMOUNTS
"Price/Unit" ---> :     $4.60       (120,000)    : <--- WILL BE TESTED
AMOUNTS           :     $4.70        (60,000)    : <---
TO BE             :     $4.80              0     :         RESULTS OF
TESTED            :     $4.90         60,000     :           TESTED
             ---> :     $5.00        120,000     :          AMOUNTS
                  :------------------------------: <---
                  ----------------------------------
```

Data Matrix Invert — /DMI

The DATA MATRIX INVERT command will copy a square matrix to a new location and invert that copy. To use this command:

1. Press the SLASH (/) key.

    The Main Menu will appear.

2. Type **D** to select **D**ata.

    The Data Menu will appear.

3. Type **M** to select **M**atrix.

    The Matrix Menu will appear.

4. Type **I** to select **I**nvert.

    The prompt "Enter range to invert" will appear.

5. Point to (or type) the range of cells to be copied.

6. Press **ENTER** to accept the range.

    The prompt "Enter output range" will appear.

7. Point to (or type) the range of cells in which the inverted matrix will appear.

8. Press **ENTER** to accept the range.

Data Matrix Multiply — /DMM

The DATA MATRIX MULTIPLY command will multiply the rows of a matrix by the columns of another matrix. The result will appear in a new location on the spreadsheet. To use this command:

1. Press the SLASH (/) key.

    The Main Menu will appear.

2. Type **D** to select **D**ata.

    The Data Menu will appear.

MISCELLANEOUS DATA COMMANDS 245

3. Type **M** to select **M**atrix.

   The Matrix Menu will appear.

4. Type **I** to select **M**ultiply.

   The prompt "Enter first range to multiply" will appear.

5. Point to (or type) the range that contains the first matrix.

6. Press **ENTER** to accept the range.

   The prompt "Enter second range to multiply" will appear.

7. Point to (or type) the range that contains the second matrix.

8. Press **ENTER** to accept the range.

   The prompt "Enter output range" will appear.

9. Point to (or type) the range of cells in which the inverted matrix will appear.

10. Press **ENTER** to accept the range.

Data Regression — /DR

The DATA REGRESSION command utilizes a statistical technique to show the relationship between different variables. The results are plotted on a line that is used to predict or forecast values.

To use the Data Regression command:

1. Press the SLASH (**/**) key.

   The Main Menu will appear.

2. Type **D** to select **D**ata.

   The Data Menu will appear.

3. Type **R** to select **R**egression.

   The Data Regression Menu and Screen will appear.

4. Type **X** to select **X** Range.

   The prompt "Enter independent variables, or X range" will appear.

5. Type or point to the range containing the independent variables (maximum of 16 columns is allowed); then press **ENTER** to accept the range.

6. Type **Y** to select **Y** Range

   The prompt "Enter dependent variable, or Y range" will appear.

7. Type or point to the range containing the independent variable; then press **ENTER** to accept the range.

   NOTE: The Y range must contain the same number of rows as the X range.

8. Type **O** to select **O**utput range.

   The prompt "Enter output range" will appear.

9. Type or point to the range that will contain output; then press **ENTER** to accept the range.

   NOTE: The output will occupy five columns by nine rows. You can either specify the entire range or only the upper left corner of the range in Step 9 above.

   NOTE: The system automatically calculates the y-axis intercept as a default. However, you set zero as the y-axis intercept by typing **I** to select **I**ntercept and then typing **Z** to select **Z**ero.

   NOTE: To clear X, Y, and Output ranges and reset the intercept to compute, type **R** to select **R**eset.

10. Type **G** to select **G**o.

MISCELLANEOUS DATA COMMANDS 247

The Data Regression Menu and screen will be cleared and the Regression Output will appear in the output range. This will contain calculated values for the Constant, Standard Error of Y value Estimates, R Squared, Number of Observations, Degrees of Freedom, the slope for each of the X Coefficients, and the Standard Error of each X Coefficient.

Data Parse — /DP

The Data Parse command will convert a column of long labels into several columns, each containing only the portion of the long label that you specify. To use Data Parse:

1. Press the SLASH (/) key.

   The Main Menu will appear.

2. Type **D** to select **D**ata.

   The Data Menu will appear.

3. Type **P** to select **P**arse.

   The Data Parse Menu and screen will appear. A format line must be set. This format will tell the system how to separate the long labels into columns.

4. To create a format line:

   a. Position the cursor over the first label to parse.

      The format line that is created will conform to the specifications that appear in that first label. This format can then be edited, if necessary.

   b. Type **F** to select **F**ormat-Line.

      The Format Line Menu will appear.

c. Type **C** to **C**reate a format line.

The format line will appear. Characters on this format line specify what type of data will appear in each parsed column.

The following characters represent the first character of a column. The column will be parsed as the data type specified:

D	Date column
L	Label column
V	Value column
T	Time column

In addition, any of these characters may appear:

S	Skip these data
>	Additional characters within column
*	Blank space in column

NOTE: For information on changing this format line, see Step 5d below.

d. Press **ENTER** to accept the format line.

5. To edit an existing format line:

    a. Position the cursor over the format line to edit.

    The format line that is created will conform to the specifications that appear in that first label. This format can then be edited, if necessary.

    b. Type **F** to select **F**ormat-Line.

    The Format Line Menu will appear.

    c. Type **E** to **E**dit the format line.

    d. Edit the format line that appears:

    - Edit line format keys can be used (**LEFT** and **RIGHT ARROWS**, **DEL** key, **BACKSPACE** key, and so on.)

MISCELLANEOUS DATA COMMANDS

- Strike over existing characters with desired characters (a list of acceptable characters appears in Step 4c above).
- **UP** or **DOWN ARROWS** can be used to move the display of the format line above or below any long label in the column.
- **PGDN** or **PGUP** keys will move the display the format line up or down one screenload in the column.
- **CTRL+BREAK** will cancel format edit and return to READY mode.
- The first time **ESC** is pressed, it will erase the format line. Subsequent presses will return the format line to its prior state.

  e. Press **ENTER** to accept the format line.

6. Type **I** to select **I**nput-Column

   The prompt "Enter column of labels to parse" will appear.

7. Type or point to the range containing the column of long labels.

   NOTE: The format line specified in Step 4 above must be included in the range.

8. Press **ENTER** to accept the column range.

9. Type **O** to select **O**utput range.

   The prompt "Enter output range" will appear.

10. Type or point to the range that will contain output; then press **ENTER** to accept the range.

    NOTE: To clear Input column and Output range, type **R** to select **R**eset.

11. Type **G** to select **G**o.

    The parsed labels appear in the specified range.

PART IV

Index

? Macro Command, 203
+/- Format, 50
@ Functions, (see "Functions")
@ Functions (example of), 27
@@, 40
\0 Macro, 160

A

ABS Function, 32
Absolute Value, 26
Access System Menu
  Diagram, M-3
  Explanation, 10
ACOS Function, 33

Add-In
  Allways, 106
  Attach, 119
  Attach as Default Setting, 122
  Clear All, 121
  Detach, 121
  Invoke, 124
  Macro Library Manager, 170–182
Advanced Macro Commands, List of, 188
Align Paper, Print Menu, 95
Allways Add-In, 106
ALT +
  F1 Key, 23
  F2, 161

F3, 164, 169
F4 Key, 72
F5 Key, 184
F7 Key, 119-120, 124
F8 Key, 119-120, 124
F9 Key, 119-120, 124
F10 Key, 119-120, 124
Annotate Macros, 167
ARROW Keys, 16
As Displayed, Print Option, 96
ASCII File Manipulation Macro Commands, 213–216
ASIN Function, 33
ATAN Function, 33
ATAN2 Function, 33
Attach
  Add-In, 119
  Add-In as Default Setting, 122
  Macro Library Manager, 170
  Macro Library Manager as Default, 173
AUTO123 Spreadsheet, 160
Autoexec Macro Defaults, 113-114
Automatic Macro Execution, 160
Automatic Recalculation, 111
AVG Function, 34

B

BACKSLASH Key
  Macros, 164
  Repeating Labels, 22
BACKSPACE Key, 19
Bar Graph, 129
Bar Graph Format, 50
Black and White, Graph, 142
BLANK Macro Command, 206
Borders, Print, 96
BORDERSON/BORDERSOFF Macro Command, 210
Bottom Margin
  Calculating, 98
  Default, Setting, 115
  Setting, 99
BRANCH
  Macro Command, 193
  DISPATCH vs subroutine, 190
Break Page, 101
BREAK Macro Command, 202
BREAKON/BREAKOFF Macro Command, 210
Built-In Functions, 28
  Example of, 27
  List of, (see "Functions")

C

CALC
  Indicator, 14
  Key, 113
Calculating
  Left/Right Margins, 97
  Top/Bottom Margins, 98
Cancel
  Learn Range, 185
  Printing, 106

INDEX

Selection of Graphs (Print), 149
CAPS Lock Indicator, 14
Cell, 15
   Address, 13, 15
   Contents in Header/Footer, 101–103
   Formulas, Print Option, 96
   Pointer, 14
   Pointer Movement, 16
CELL Function, 41
CELLPOINTER Function, 41
Center Labels, 21
CHAR Function, 35
Characters, Composing, 23
Chart, Pie, 131
CHOOSE Function, 42
CIRC Indicator, 14
CLEAN Function, 35
Clear
   All Add-Ins, 121
   All Add-Ins (Macro Library Manager), 172
   /Lock Titles, 60
   Margins, 105
   Print Options, 104
Clock Display Defaults, Setting, 117
CLOSE Macro Command, 214
CMD Indicator, 14
CODE Function, 35
Color,
   Graph, 142
   Range, (Graph), 154
COLS Function, 42

Column, 15
   Delete, 65
   Hide/Display, 59
   Insert, 67
   Width, Global, 58
   Width, One Column, 56
   Width, Range of Columns, 57
Columnwise Recalculation, 111
Combine Files, 79
Comma Format, 49
Command Structure, 3
Compose Key, 23
Constructing Macros, 163–169
CONTENTS Macro Command, 206
Control Environment, Macros, 210–212
Control Panel, 13
Convert Files, 91–93
Copy, 68
Correcting Errors, 19
COUNT Function, 34
Create
   Data Table, 239
   Range Name, 108
Criteria
   Range, 223–229
   Range Headings, 223, 225, 228
   Specifying, 230
CTERM Function, 30
CTRL+
   ARROW Keys, 17
   BREAK Keys to Cancel Printing, 106
Currency
   Format, 49

Symbol Default, Setting, 117
Current Graph, 127
Cursor Movement, 16

D

Data
Distribution, 239
Fill, 238
Labels, Graph, 136
Matrix
Invert, 244
Multiply, 244
Menu Selections, 221
Parse, 247
Query
Delete, 228
Extract, 225
Find, 223
Reset, 229
Unique, 227
Range, 233
Group, 132
Bar/Stacked-Bar/Line Graph, 129
Pie Chart, 131
XY Graph, 130
Regression, 245
Sort Reset, 235
Table
Create, 239
Key, 241
Reset, 241
Database, 220-237
Data Queries, 223-232
Delete Records, 228
Extract Records, 225
Extract Unique Records, 227
Find Records, 223
General Information, 220-222
QUERY Key, 230
Reset Data Query, 229
Sort Records, 233-235
Specifying Criteria, 230
Statistical Functions, 236-237
Date
Format, 51
Format Default Setting, 117
Function, Using, 30
Functions,
List/Definition, 28-29
in Header/Footer, 101-102
DATEVALUE Function, 29
DAVG Function, 236
DAY Function, 28
DCOUNT Function, 236
DDB Function, 30
Debugging Macros, 217
Default
Autoexecute Macro, 160
Directory, Change, 83
Global, 113-119
Print Settings, 97
Setting, Attach Macro Library Manager, 173
DEFINE Macro Command, 194
Delete
Named Graph, 144-145
Range Name, 108
Records, 228
Row/Column, 65

Detach
  Add-In, 121
  Macro Library Manager, 172
Directory
  Change Default, 83
  Defaults, 113-114
  Graph, Changing, 154
Disable
  Global Protection, 62
  Undo, 72
  Undo, Default Setting, 117
Disk
  Handling, 7
  Protection, 8
  Storage, 76-90
DISPATCH
  Macro Command, 194
  vs BRANCH vs subroutine, 190
Display/Hide Columns, 59
Distribution, Frequency, 239
DMAX Function, 236
DMIN Function, 236
Drive, Change Default, 83
DSTD Function, 236
DSUM Function, 236
DVAR Function, 236

E

Edit
  Key, 19-20
  Macro Library File, 178
EDIT Mode Indicator, 13
Editing, 64-75
Eject Paper (Graph Print), 153

Enable
  Global Protection, 62
  Undo, 72
  Undo, Default Setting, 117
END
  + ARROW Keys, 16-17
  + HOME Keys, 16
  Indicator, 14
Environment, Macro Commands, 210-212
Erase
  Contents of Learn Range, 185
  File, 83
  Range, 66
  Worksheet, 64
ERR Function, 42
Error Correction, 19
ERROR Mode Indicator, 14
ESC Key, 6
EXACT Function, 35
Exit
  System, 12
  Temporarily to Operating System, 11
EXP Function, 32
Extract
  File, 81
  Records, 225
  Unique Records, 227

F

F1 Key, 6
F2 Key, 19-20
F3 Key, 5
F4 Key, 26
F5 Key, 18

F6 Key, 61
F7 Key, 230
F8 Key, 241
F9 Key, 113
F10 Key, 127
  When printing graphs, 149
FALSE Function, 39
Field, 220
  Name, 220
File
  Change Default Directory, 83
  Combine, 79
  Directory, Graph, Changing, 154
  Erase, 83
  Extract, 81
  Import, 86
  Link, 88
  List, 83
  Manipulation Macro Commands, 213–216
  Refresh Link, 89
  Reservation, 89
  Retrieve, 78
  Save, 76
  Table, 87
FILES Mode Indicator, 13
FILESIZE Macro Command, 215
Fill Data, 238
Financial Functions
  List/Definition, 30–31
  Using, 31–32
Find Records, 223
FIND
  Function, 36
  Mode Indicator, 13

First Title, Graph, 137
Fixed Format, 48
Font Directory, Graph, Changing, 154
Footer/Header, 101
FOR Macro Command, 196
FORBREAK Macro Command, 196
Format, 45–63
  +/-, 50
  Comma, 49
  Currency, 49
  Date, 51
  Fixed, 48
  General, 50
  Global, 45
  Graph, 135
  Hidden, 52
  Menu Selections, 47
  Percent, 50
  Print Option, 96
  Range, 46
  Reset, 52
  Scientific, 48
  Text, 52
Formulas
  Search, 73
  Search and Replace, 74
  Typing, 24
FRAMEON/FRAMEOFF Macro Command, 210
Frequency Distribution, 239
FRMT Mode Indicator, 14
Front (Graph Print), 152
Function Key
  ALT + F1, 23
  ALT + F2, 161
  ALT + F3, 164, 169
  ALT + F4, 72
  ALT + F5, 184

INDEX

ALT + F7, 119-120, 124
ALT + F8, 119-120, 124
ALT + F9, 119-120, 124
ALT + F10, 119-120, 124
F1, 6
F2, 19–20
F3, 5
F4, 26
F5, 18
F6, 61
F7, 230
F8, 241
F9, 113
F10, 127
F10 (when printing graphs), 149
List of, 17
in Macros, 166
Functions, 28–44
@@, 40
@ABS, 32
@ACOS, 33
@ACOS, 33
@ASIN, 33
@ATAN, 33
@ATAN2, 33
@AVG, 34
@CELL, 41
@CELLPOINTER, 41
@CHAR, 35
@CHOOSE, 42
@CLEAN, 35
@CODE, 35
@COLS, 42
@COUNT, 34
@CTERM, 30
@DATEVALUE, 29
@DAVG, 236
@DAY, 28
@DCOUNT, 236
@DDB, 30
@DMAX, 236
@DMIN, 236
@DSTD, 236
@DSUM, 236
@DVAR, 236
@ERR, 42
@EXACT, 35
@EXP, 32
@FALSE, 39
@FIND, 36
@FV, 30
@HLOOKUP, 42
@IF, 39
@INDEX, 43
@INT, 32
@IRR, 30
@ISAAF, 39
@ISAAP, 39
@ISERR, 39
@ISNA, 39
@ISNUMBER, 39
@ISSTRING, 40
@LEFT, 36
@LENGTH, 36
@LN, 32
@LOG, 32
@LOWER, 36
@MAX, 34
@MID, 36
@MIN, 34
@MOD, 32
@MONTH, 28
@N, 37
@NA, 43
@NOW, 29
@NPV, 31
@PI, 33
@PMT, 31
@PROPER, 37

@PV, 31
@RAND, 32
@RATE, 31
@REPEAT, 37
@REPLACE, 37
@RIGHT, 37
@ROUND, 33
@ROWS, 43
@S, 37
@SIN, 33
@SLN, 31
@SQRT, 33
@STD, 34
@STRING, 37
@SUM, 34
@SYD, 31
@TAN, 33
@TERM, 31
@TIMEVALUE, 29
@TRIM, 38
@TRUE, 40
@UPPER, 38
@VALUE, 38
@VAR, 34
@VLOOKUP, 43
@YEAR, 28
Functions,
Database Statistical, 236–237
Date, List/Definition, 28–29
Date, Using, 30
Financial, List/Definition, 30–31
Financial, Using, 31–32
Logical, List/Description, 39–40
Logical, Using, 40
Mathematical, List/Definition, 32–33
Mathematical, Using, 33–34
Special, List/Description, 40–43
Special, Using, 43–44
Statistical, List/Definitions, 34–35
Statistical, Using, 34–35
String, List/Definitions, 35–38
String, Using, 38
Time, List/Definition, 28–29
Time, Using, 30
Trigonometric, List/Definitions, 33
Trigonometric, Using, 33–34
FV 30

G

General
Format, 50
Information, 3
GET Macro Command, 203
GETLABEL Macro Command, 203
GETNUMBER Macro Command, 204
GETPOS Macro Command, 216
Global
Column Width, 58
Defaults, 113–119

Attach Macro Library Manager, 173
Autoexecute Macro, 160
Format, 45
Label Prefix, 53
Protection, 62
Suppression of Zeros, 54
Globally Enable/Disable Undo, 72
Go, Print Menu, 95
GoTo Key, 18
Graph
Bar, 129
Current, 127
Key, 127
Line, 129
Menu, 126
Name, 144
Options, 134-142
Pie, 131
Printing, 147-159
Reset, 128
Save, 143
Save vs Name, 145
Size, 150
Storage, 143-146
Type, 132
View, 127
XY, 130
Graphics, 126-159
GRAPHON/GRAPHOFF Macro Command, 210
Grid (Graph), 134
Group Data Range, 132

H

Header/Footer, 101
Help, 6

Help Defaults, Setting, 117
HELP Mode Indicator, 14
Hidden Format, 52
Hide/Display Columns, 59
HLOOKUP Function, 42
HOME Key, 16
Horizontal
Bar Graph Format, 50
Titles, Lock/Clear, 60
Split Windows, 61

I

IF Function, 39
IF Macro Command, 197
Import File, 86
INDEX Function, 43
INDICATE Macro Command, 211
Input, 19
Correcting Errors During, 19
Formulas, 24
Labels, 20
Macro Commands that Wait for User-, 203–205
Range, 108
Range, 223–228
Values, 24
INS Key, 15
Insert Row/Column, 67
Install Software, 9
INT Function, 32
Interface (Printer) Defaults, Setting, 115
Interface, Printer, Graph, 157
International Default, Setting, 117

Invert Data Matrix, 244
Invoke
  Add-In, 124
  Macro Library Manager, 175
IRR Function, 30
ISAAF Function, 39
ISAAP Function, 39
ISERR Function, 39
ISNA Function, 39
ISNUMBER Function, 39
ISSTRING Function, 40
Iteration, 111

J

Justification in Header/Footer, 101–103
Justify
  Labels, 21
  Range, 55

K

Keys, 233

L

Label
  Data, Graph, 136
  Macro, 164, 167
  Name,@sub - 108
  Prefixes, 21
  Range Name, 108
  Repeating, 22
  Search, 73
  Search and Replace, 74
  Typing, 20
LABEL Mode Indicator, 14
Label-Prefix
  Format Global Setting, 53
  Format Range of, 52
Learn Macro, 183–185
  Range, Specify, 183
  Range, Cancel, 185
  Range, Erase Contents, 185
LEARN Key, 184
Left
  Margin Default,Setting, 115
  Margin, Setting/Calculating, 97
LEFT Function, 36
Left-Justify Labels, 21
Legend, Graph, 137
Length, Page, Setting, 100
LENGTH Function, 36
LET Macro Command, 207
Library Manger, Macro, 170–182
Line
  Advance, Print Menu, 95
  Graph, 129
Linking Files, 88
  Files, Refresh, 89
List
  Files, 83
  Names of Macros in Current Library File, 181
LN Function, 32
Load Macro Library File, 180
Lock/Clear Titles, 60
LOCK Indicators, 14

LOG Function, 32
Logical Functions
　List/Description, 39–40
　Using, 40
LOOK Macro Command, 205
Looping and Calling Macro Commands, 190–198
LOWER Function, 36

M

Macro, 160-217
　Commands
　　Advanced, List of, 188
　　Controlling Environment, 210–212
　　Looping and Calling, 190–198
　　Spreadsheet Manipulation, 206–209
　　Suspension, 202
　　Text File Manipulation, 213–216
　　User-Defined Menus, 199–201
　　User-Input, 203–205
　　/X, 186–187
　Debugging, 217
　Learn Feature, 183–185
　　Cancel Range, 185
　　Erase Contents of Range, 185
　　Specify Range, 183
　Library Manager, 170–182
　　Detach, 172
　　Edit Macro, 178
　　Invoke Macro, 175
　　List Macro Names in Current File, 181
　　Load Macro, 180
　　Remove File, 181
　　Save Macro, 177
　Planning/Construction, 163–169
　Tips, 217
Manipulate Spreadsheet, Macro Commands, 206–209
Manual Recalculation, 111
Margins
　Clear, 105
　Defaults, Setting, 115
　Left/Right, Calculating/Setting, 97
　Top/Bottom
　　Calculating, 98
　　Setting, 99
Mathematical Functions
　List/Definition, 32–33
　Functions, Using, 33–34
Matrix, Data
　Invert, 244
　Multiply, 244
MAX Function, 34
MEM Indicator, 14
Menu, User-Defined Macro Commands, 199–201
MENU Mode Indicator, 13
MENUBRANCH
　Macro Command, 199
　vs MENUCALL, 200
MENUCALL
　Macro Command, 200
　vs MENUBRANCH, 200

Menus, 3
MID Function, 36
MIN Function, 34
MOD Function, 32
Mode Indicators, 13
MONTH Function, 28
Move, 70
Move Pointer, 16
Multiply Data Matrix, 244
Multiuser Environment,
 File Reservation, 89

N

N Function, 37
NA Function, 43
Name
 Graph, 144
 Key, 5
 Macro, 167
 Range, 108
NAME Mode Indicator, 13
Names of Macros in Current
 Library File, 181
Natural Recalculation, 111
Negative Number Display
 Default, Setting, 117
NOW Function, 29
NPV Function, 31
NUM Lock Indicator, 15
Numbering Pages, 101–102

O

ONERROR Macro
 Command, 195
OPEN Macro Command, 213
Operating System,
 Temporarily Exit to, 11

Operators, 24–25
Options
 Graph, 134-142
 Print, Clear, 104
Other Print Options, 96
Output Range Headings,
 225
OVR Lock Indicator, 15

P

Page
 Advance, Print Menu, 95
 Break, 101
 Length
  Default, Setting, 115
  Setting, 100
 Numbering, 101–102
PANELON/PANELOFF
 Macro Command, 211
Paper Size, Graph, 157
Parse Data, 247
Path, Change Default, 83
Pause Printing (Graph), 154
Percent Format, 50
PG DN Key, 17
PG UP Key, 17
PI Function, 33
Pie Chart, 131
Planning Macros, 163–169
PMT Function, 31
POINT Mode Indicator, 13
Pointer Movement, 16
Prefixes, Labels, 21
Primary Key, 233
Print, 94–107
 Add-Ins, Allways, 106
 Calculate Top/Bottom
  Margins, 98

Cancel, 106
Command, General
    Information, 94
Default Settings, 97
Graph, 147-159
Header/Footer, 101
Menu Selections, 95
Options, Clear, 104
Options Menu Selections,
    95–96
Set/Calculate Left/Right
    Margins, 97
Set Page Length, 100
Set Top/Bottom Margins,
    99
Settings (Graph), 149
Setup Strings, 101
Printer
Defaults, 113-115
Select, Graph, 156
Setup Strings, 103
PRTSC Key, 83
PROPER Function, 37
Protect Disk, 8
**Protect/Unprotect,
    Range, 63**
Protection, Global, 62
**Punctuation Default,
    Setting, 117**
PUT Macro Command, 208
PV Function, 31

Q

Queries, Data, 223–232
QUERY Key, 230
Quit 1-2-3, 11
QUIT Macro Command, 202

R

RAND Function, 32
Range
Colors, (Graph), 154
Data, Bar/Stacked-Bar/
    Line Graph, 129
Data, Group, 132
Data, Pie Chart, 131
Data, XY Graph, 130
Erase, 66
Format, 46
Input, 108
Justify, 55
Label-Prefix, 52
Learn, Cancel, 185
Learn, Erase Contents,
    185
Name, 108
Name (in Macros), 167
Name, Create, Delete,
    Labels, Reset, 108
Name Table, 110
of Columns, Set/Reset
    Width, 57
Print, 95
Protect/Unprotect, 63
Search, 18
Search, 73
Search and Replace, 74
Specify, 4
Specify (for Copy and
    Move), 71
Specify Macro Learn, 183
Transpose, 69
Value, 68
RATE Function, 31
Re-Set Defaults, 113-119
**READ Macro Command,
    214**

READLN Macro Command, 214
READY Mode Indicator, 13
RECALC Macro Command, 208
RECALCCOL Macro Command, 209
Recalculation
  Automatic, 111
  Columnwise/Rowwise, 111
  Iteration, 111
  Manual, 111
  Natural, 111
  Worksheet Global, 111
Record, 220
Record Macro Keystrokes, 184
Refresh File Link, 89
Regression, Data, 245
Remove Macro Library File, 181
REPEAT Function, 37
Repeating Labels, 22
Replace Range, 74
REPLACE Function, 37
Reservation, File, 89
Reset
  Column Width
    One Column, 56
    Range of Columns, 57
  Data
    Query, 229
    Sort, 235
    Table, 241
  Format, 52
  Graph, 128
    Print, 158
  Range Name, 108

RESTART Macro Command, 195
Retrieve File, 78
RETURN Macro Command, 193
Revise Cell Contents, 64–75
Right Margin
  Default, Setting, 115
  Setting/Calculating, 97
RIGHT Function, 37
Right-Justify Labels, 21
ROUND Function, 33
Row/Column
  Delete, 65
  Insert, 67
Rows, 15
ROWS Function, 43
Rowwise Recalculation, 111
RUN (Macro) Key, 164, 169

S

S Function, 37
Save File, 76
Save
  Graph, 143
  Macro Library File, 177
  Print Settings, Graph, 159
Scale
  Skip, Graph, 141
  X-/Y-Axis, Graph, 137
Scientific Format, 48
Screen Orientation, 13
SCROLL LOCK
  Indicator, 15
  Key, 16
Scrolling, 16

Search
   and Replace Range, 74
   Range, 18, 73
Second Title, Graph, 137
Secondary Key, 233
Select
   Graph To Print, 149
   Printer, Graph, 156
Set
   Defaults, 113-119
   Column Width
      Global, 58
      One Column, 56
      Range of Columns, 57
Set Up Database, 220
SETPOS Macro Command, 216
Setting
   Left/Right Margins, 97
   Page Length, 100
   Top/Bottom Margins, 99
   Print Defaults, 97
   Print, Graph, 149
Setup String
   Default, Setting, 115
   Printer, 103
SHIFT + PRTSC Key, 83
SHIFT + TAB Key, 17
SIN Function, 33
Size
   Graph, 150
   Paper, Graph, 157
Skip, Scale, Graph, 141
SLN Function, 31
Sort
   Order, 233-234
   Reset, 235
Sorting Records, 233-235
Special Functions
   List/Description, 40-43

   Using, 43-44
Specify
   Criteria, 230
   Macro Learn Range, 183
   Range, 4
   Range (for Copy and Move), 71
Split Windows, 61
Spreadsheet
   Manipulation Macro Commands, 206-209
   Recalculation, 111
SQRT Function, 33
SST Indicator, 15
Stacked-Bar
   Graph, 129
   Bar, 129
Start System, 9
Statistical Functions
   List/Definitions, 34
   Using, 34
Status, Worksheet, 111
STATUS Mode Indicator, 14
STD Function, 34
Step Execution, 161
STEP Indicator, 15
STEP Key, 161
Stop Printing, 106
Storage, 76-90
   Graph, 143-146
String (Setup) Default, Setting, 115
String Functions
   List/Definitions, 35-38
   Using, 38
STRING Function, 37
Strings, Printer Setup, 103
Subroutine
   Macro Command, 191

vs BRANCH vs DISPATCH, 190
SUM
 Formula Construction, 27
 Function, 34
Suppress Display of Zeros, 54
Suspend Macro, 202
SYD Function, 31
System
 Exit to, 12
 Startup, 9
 Temporarily Exit to, 11
SYSTEM Macro Command, 198

T

TAB Key, 17
Table
 Data
  Create, 239
  Reset, 241
 of Files, 87
 of Graphs, 144-145
 Range Name, 110
TABLE Key, 241
TAN Function, 33
Template Construction
TERM Function, 31
Text
 File Manipulation Macro Commands, 213-216
 Format, 52
Tilde Key (in Macros), 166
Time Format Default, Setting, 117
Time Functions
 List/Definition, 28-29
 Using, 30
TIME Function, 29
TIMEVALUE Function, 29
Titles
 Graph, 137
 Lock/Unlock, 60
Top Margins
 Calculating, 98
 Setting, 99
 Defaults Setting, 115
Translate Files, 91-93
Transpose Range, 69
Trigonometric Functions
 List/Definitions, 33
 Using, 33-34
TRIM Function, 38
TRUE Function, 40
Type, Graph, 132
 Bar, 129
 Line, 129
 Pie, 131
 Stack-Bar 129
 XY, 130
Typing
 Formulas, 24
 Information, 19
 Labels, 20
 Macros, 163-169
 Values, 24

U

Undo
 Disable/Enable, 72
 Feature Default, Setting, 117
 Key, 72
UNDO Indicator, 15

INDEX

Unformatted, Print Option, 96
Unique Records, Extract, 227
Unlock/Lock Titles, 60
Unprotect/Protect, Range, 63
UPPER Function, 38
Use
  Add-In, 124
  Graph, 144
  Macro, 169
User Input Macro Command, 203–205
User-Defined Menu Macro Commands, 199–201

V

Value
  Absolute, 26
  Range Copy, 68
  Typing, 24
VALUE
  Function, 38
  Mode Indicator, 14
VAR Function, 34
Vertical
  Split Windows, 61
  Titles, Lock/Clear, 60
View Graph, 127
VLOOKUP Function, 43

W

WAIT
  Macro Command, 202
  Mode Indicator, 14
WINDOW Key, 61
Windows, 61
WINDOWSON/WINDOWSOFF Macro Command, 212
Worksheet
  Erase, 64
  Global
    Defaults, 113-119
    Format, 45
    Recalculation, 111
  Grid, 15
  Protection, 62
  Status, 111
WRITE Macro Command, 215
Write-Protect, 8
WRITELN Macro Command, 215
Writing Macros, 163–169

X

/X Macro Commands, 186–187
X-axis Scale, Graph, 137
X-axis Title, Graph, 137
/XC Command, 192
/XC Command vs /XG Command, 190
/XG Command, 193
/XI Command, 197
/XL Command, 203
/XM Command, 199
/XN Command, 204
/XQ Command, 202
/XR Command, 193

Xtract File, 81
XY Graph, 130

Y

Y-axis Scale, Graph, 137

Y-Axis, Graph, 137
YEAR Function, 28

Z

Zero Suppression Format, 54